Literacy
Through
Symbols

SECOND EDITION

Literacy Through Symbols

Improving access
for children and adults

SECOND EDITION

Tina Detheridge and Mike Detheridge

David Fulton Publishers
London

MT

David Fulton Publishers Ltd
The Chiswick Centre, 414 Chiswick High Road, London W4 5TF

www.fultonpublishers.co.uk

Copyright © Tina Detheridge and Mike Detheridge 2002

British Library Cataloguing in Publication Data
A catalogue record for this book is available from the British Library

ISBN 1–85346–852–5

Typeset by Elite Typesetting Techniques Ltd., Eastleigh, Hampshire, UK
Printed in Great Britain by Bell and Bain Ltd, Glasgow

3/1/04

Contents

This book is dedicated to Judy van Oosterom for her innovative work in the early days of symbol use, and for her ongoing infectious enthusiasm and unfailing support.

Acknowledgements

Our first and particular thanks must go to two people without whose influence we would never have started on symbols. Robin Beste first suggested we work on symbols while developing computer programs for the BBC computer, and Judy van Oosterom who has always had the forward vision to see the wide application of symbols and to understand the power that computer technology has to offer even, as she herself would admit, at a somewhat advancing age!

We have worked with so many people on symbols who have freely and willingly talked to us about ideas and contributed them to this book. It would be impossible to thank them all individually and we hope we will be forgiven for not doing so. We are especially grateful to the symbol users and teachers who have given us material to reproduce. We must, however, single out just a few whose help and assistance have been inestimable. These are Clare Martin and Bernard Gummett from George Hastwell School in Cumbria, Gill Lloyd from Woodlands School in Surrey and Dave Wood and the staff at Wilson Stuart School in Birmingham. Clare and Bernard have given us so many ideas and feedback over the years, Gill works with 16–19-year-olds and her perspective and thoughtful approach have greatly influenced our own thinking, and Dave and his staff have given very practical ideas on using symbols with young children.

Since the publication of the first edition of *Literacy Through Symbols*, Chris Abbott has continued documenting symbol use in *Symbols Now* (2000), and we are grateful to the contributors to that book who have given their permission for material to be reproduced in this revision.

Thanks are also due to Gillian Hazell of the ACE Centre, Oxford, for advice on the variety of symbol systems; and to the Makaton Vocabulary Development Project for permission to reproduce the curriculum examples relating to Figures 3.2, 6.7 and 8.8, and to the many other contributors who have allowed us to reproduce their materials.

Finally, our grateful thanks to Barry Carpenter for writing the Foreword to this book. Perhaps more importantly, thanks are also due to Barry for setting up the Getting it Clear conference at Westminster College, Oxford, back in 1996, which was really the starting point for this book, and for his continued encouragement.

Foreword

What is the price of a dream not dreamed?
What is the price of a word not spoken?
What is the price of a voice not heard?
What is the price of a vision not imagined?
What is the price of a life not lived?

Michael Williams
An augmentative communication user

I used these words to end the Foreword to the first edition of *Literacy Through Symbols*, as a reflective point for practitioners. As I read them again I am struck by the enabling properties of symbols. They enable dreams to be dreamed, and visions to be realised; they enable words to be spoken so that others might hear. Most of all they improve the quality of life for so many people with special needs. Symbols are truly a liberating device.

The generative nature of symbols is evidenced by the increasing range of diverse practice that has emerged since the first edition of this book. These developments have happened within an ever-changing agenda, and amidst a sea of new initiatives. In the first edition, Tina and Mike Detheridge brought together a range of exemplar material to make a case for symbol use. This edition affirms, from a confident stance, the undeniable contribution symbols can make to the teaching, learning and daily life experiences of children and adults with special needs. The examples taken directly from symbol users are powerful testimony to how symbols have enriched their lives. They have empowered people with a range of disabilities to be a part of this world, and not apart from it.

The range of technologies which now exist to support the symbol user are breathtaking. When the authors referred to the wonderful contribution of Judy van Oosterom to the development of symbols in the UK, I could not help but recall those days back in 1985 when representatives from the Rebus and Makaton organisations would meet to devise symbols fitting to the UK context. In those days you drew symbols by hand; they were then cut and pasted into workbooks, textbooks, onto displays and worksheets. Look how far we have come! The technological advances are remarkable, but they are worthless unless they are accessible. Accessible to the symbol user, child or adult, yes; but also to those responsible for devising symbols-based materials and programmes – the practitioners. In this respect the contribution of Tina and Mike Detheridge has been outstanding. They have given practitioners high-quality, accessible programmes with which their creative talents have been unleashed on this dynamic medium. The exemplars in this book illustrate this time and time again.

The context for literacy has changed since the first edition. For adults with learning disabilities, the greater emphasis on independent living and self-advocacy strategies (Mittler 2001) that support community living and access to services, are vital to the quality of life of people with learning disabilities. Symbols are 'community-friendly'. They exist for all of us as a means of quick and easy information-giving. Thus for people with disabilities they are merely an extension and elaboration of this everyday graphic medium.

The National Literacy Strategy in schools has considerably raised the profile of literacy in the curriculum. Schools, in seeking to differentiate their literacy curriculum to embrace all learners, have found symbols an effective medium for so doing (Carpenter and Morris 2001).

Inclusion is an all-embracing societal concept. It is heartening to read in the Inclusion Statement which prefaces the National Curriculum 2000, that symbols are openly recognised as a facilitating medium for access to the curriculum. The subsequent publication of *Planning, Teaching and Assessing the Curriculum for Pupils with Learning Difficulties* (DfES/QCA 2001), places symbols at the heart of the assessment process in the learning outcomes articulated in the 'P' levels.

In just over a decade, symbols have moved from being peripheral to the daily learning experience of people with learning disabilities (available to only a few in specialist settings), to an integral part of their lives, whether in school or community settings. This second edition of *Literacy Through Symbols* makes a seminal contribution to sustaining the profile of symbols.

Barry Carpenter OBE
Chief Executive
Sunfield School
Worcestershire

Introduction

This book describes how symbols can support the learning, communication and autonomy of many people. The focus is very much on an inclusive view of special needs. It encompasses those students and people who will always find reading and writing text very difficult, together with the very many who will master this process but who need some additional help. This book will, therefore, be useful for teachers, therapists, parents, carers, social workers and anyone who comes into daily contact with those for whom symbols may be useful. The book will be of value to managers who need to be sure that, in this area, they have internalised the issues of accessible information.

Most of the background development in symbols has been in the area of Alternative and Augmentative Communication for people with severe speech difficulties. The role of graphical symbols focused on their use in augmenting speech and direct face-to-face communication. In more recent years symbols have been used by people with learning difficulties in wider contexts, in education, in advocacy, in accessing information and in facilitating the users' own written communication.

This book looks at this much wider role for symbol use, and will show an extensive range of current practical applications. Although a great deal of development has taken place since the first edition of this book in 1997, the literature on symbol use is not extensive. Little research has taken place on the role of symbols to support literacy. The intention of this book is to provide an introduction to the topic by reviewing current practice. It cannot, however, present any formal answers backed up by academic research.

As with any educational development, the use of symbols raises many questions and issues and we hope this book will provide a stimulus for discussion. It is practical, drawing on work taking place in schools, colleges and adult centres. It is illustrated with examples and ideas which demonstrate how symbols might help some pupils, students and adults.

Chapter 1 describes the background to current symbol use, who is using symbols and the pressures that are currently acting in favour of this development. Chapter 2 looks at the nature of symbols and describes one of the symbol systems in use, in order to give the reader an insight into the structure of graphical communication. Chapter 3 explores issues of introducing symbols and Chapter 4 looks at how symbols might support or enhance access to literacy. Chapter 5 looks specifically at the use of symbols within the curriculum in schools and Chapter 6 discusses the use of symbols to support independence, with particular focus on the use of symbols with older students and users. Chapter 7 discusses some of the issues of making information accessible and how symbols might assist, and, finally, Chapter 8 looks back at the issues that were uppermost in our minds when the first edition of this book was published in 1997, discusses how these issues have changed and identifies some of the current concerns.

Tina Detheridge
Mike Detheridge
Leamington Spa
April 2002

1 ■ Symbols for all

This is a book about pictorial symbols which are used to help children, young people and adults who have difficulty using standard text. The focus is upon the use of symbols to support literacy, rather than their role in facilitating direct, face-to-face communication, although there is a great deal of overlap between the two areas.

The use of symbols has been steadily growing since the early 1980s. In 1997 we wrote that there had recently been a quiet revolution in their use, and this has continued. This chapter shows some of the ways in which symbols have had an impact on learners, presents the context for the recent growth in the use of symbols, and traces the historical development of symbols, focusing on pictorial systems.

1. Where we are

Literacy is '1. The ability to read and write. 2. The ability to use language proficiently' (*Collins Dictionary of English Usage* 1980). There are many pupils, students and adults in society who have difficulties with literacy. It is a concern of government, and more importantly of all educators and carers of those people with such difficulties. This book is primarily about people who have difficulty grasping some of the initial concepts of reading and writing or who have more serious learning difficulties.

The increase in concern for people with literacy difficulties has gained new impetus as a result of recent legislative changes. The introduction of the National Curriculum in England and Wales in 1989 had a particular impact on pupils with severe learning difficulties by encouraging schools to expand their ethos from one of mainly care, to one which provides more emphasis on education. The *Code of Practice on the Identification and Assessment of Special Educational Needs* (DFE 1994) focused schools' attention on meeting individual needs of pupils in schools. More recent changes in provision for adults with learning difficulties from institutional to community care has prompted many organisations to reappraise the opportunities for their members. It was not until 1970 that the provision for pupils with severe learning difficulties was managed by the education authorities. This means that many adults now in their forties or older, have 'missed out' on education and are only just starting to develop a sense of autonomy and self-worth. Current disability legislation indicates the rights of individuals to information. Access to literacy through symbols is one of the ways of enhancing this development.

1

2. Who is using symbols?

Some stories about children and young people who have begun to use symbols will help to set the scene. The first illustrations demonstrate the impact that symbols are making in the adult community because this is a comparatively new and rapidly developing area. Other examples follow, which show the wide range of situations where symbols are being used to help those experiencing difficulties with reading.

Mike, a young adult living in the community

Mike is a young adult living in a house in the community with support of carers. His mother, Johanna, has been using symbols with him to maintain strong family links and to help Mike to share his enthusiasms and experience more effectively with those around him. Mike uses a Polaroid camera. When something happens that he wants to share, he will take a photograph or two. At the weekends, when Mike and Johanna meet up, they work together to create a story about the event. On family outings digital photos are frequently taken. Afterwards Mike and his parents write a story for Mike to share with others. A carer also has helped Mike to write stories and make schedules.

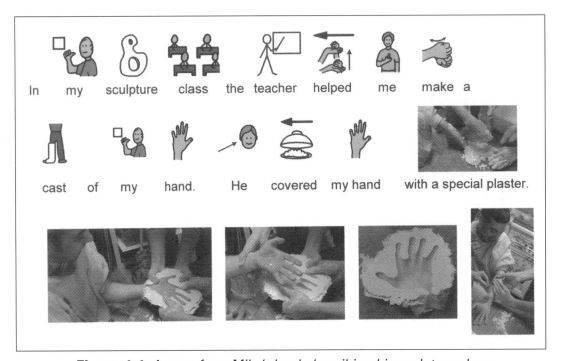

Figure 1.1 A page from Mike's book describing his sculpture class

   These pages are all added to a life history book that will gradually build up a record of Mike's life and that of his family (Figure 1.1). As well as helping Mike to remember these people and events, the book is a great help when Mike is with the carers where he lives, helping them to know more about Mike and his conversations.
   Mike also likes to work independently, using a grid of symbols of familiar topics to view symbols, to listen to the words spoken that are associated with the symbols

and to print the symbols in which he is interested. Sometimes he shares what he prints with his carers. Mike keeps the printouts in a notebook that he maintains.

Mike, who lives in the USA, uses this technique to correspond with family members who live out of town, and has recently started to write letters to a friend in the UK. It is a new departure to be able to communicate at a distance with somebody you have never met. It shows the power of symbols in widening horizons as well as maintaining current friendships.

Mike's friend in the UK is Rebecca. They correspond by letter. Rebecca lives in the UK and like Mike, has a great deal of family support, but is making enormous strides using symbols to support her communication and learning. She uses a communication book (Figures 6.2 and 6.3) which has opened channels for communicating with new people and increasing her independence.

Not all students take to symbols as easily as Mike, but for many people symbols can provide very significant help. For some people it may provide their only access to written information. For the large group of people with learning disabilities and other non-literate adults, symbols can provide a means to increased independence, making genuine choices, and expressing opinions, all of which contribute towards a more integrated lifestyle.

Alan, a young man at a school for pupils with severe learning difficulties

When we met Alan he was 17, in the senior class at school. He told us a story about how his bike had been stolen. This story was full of detail, and told in a clear sequence. The best part was how the local newspaper found out about it, came to take his photo and then put it in the paper. As a result of this, his bike was found. A year earlier Alan would not have been able to repeat that story with such clarity so long after the event. His teacher believed that Alan had been helped to recall the events because he had written about them.

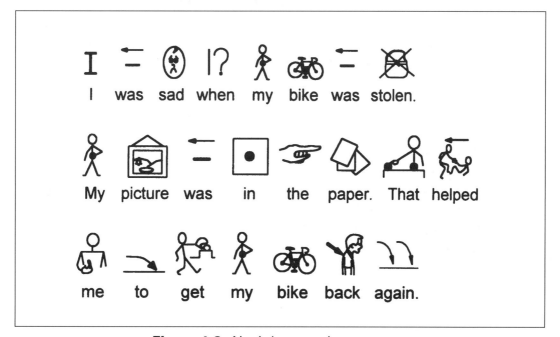

Figure 1.2 Alan's letter to the newspaper

Many of us use writing as a means of helping us to remember. We make notes, lists and write reminders. Often it is the very process of writing that helps to fix those ideas in our minds. Writing can help us to structure information, and gives another means of articulating ideas. Writing is important not just for communicating ideas, but it also helps in developing memory. This process is as important for people with learning disabilities as it is for those with good literacy skills. In fact, it can be argued that it is even more important for people with learning disabilities because they often have major problems in remembering verbal information.

Mechanisms are needed whereby non-writers can have a means of engaging in this process. The ways in which symbol users can write, together with illustrations of the many uses of symbols in adult contexts, are given throughout the book.

Peter, finding life difficult in an ordinary school

Peter, aged 9, had some severe difficulties in taking part in the school curriculum. In particular, he had difficulty acquiring reading skills. His sight vocabulary was very limited. He had mild ataxia, affecting his control of fine movement and making handwriting very difficult. He also had very quiet and indistinct speech, making it difficult to hear him in a busy classroom. The consequence of these difficulties was to make life very hard for Peter. He seemed to fall behind at every step, even though he made great efforts. His learning support teacher decided to try to help him with symbols. Initially his class teacher was reluctant: There was quite a lot of resistance to this by the class teacher. This was not something that any other child used, and she felt that it would create more problems than it solved. However, during some personal tuition sessions, the support teacher helped Peter to write some stories about familiar events and things that happened to him. After that they started to write about other topics that interested him.

Peter gained a lot of satisfaction from making these books, and was proud to take them back to his class teacher. The fact that Peter was able to read his writing back to the class teacher convinced her to let him use symbols as part of his regular classroom strategy. Another incidental gain was the pleasure that Peter's parents got from seeing some high quality work coming home from school for the first time.

Symbols in primary schools

Pupils like Peter are often helped by the pictorial support which symbols can give in early reading activities. Joan Robson, from the Surrey MLD (Moderate Learning Difficulties) Support Service, has made a bank of symbol materials to support the stories from the various reading schemes used in her area. She has made paper overlays for the overlay keyboard (Figure 4.1), to help pupils to write about the stories they had read. These materials encouraged further reading, increasing sight vocabulary and comprehension.

Figure 1.3 *An overlay to encourage writing about a story*

Shirley Austin uses symbols with her pupils who have behavioural difficulties. These work cards are designed to help the pupils think about their feelings and behaviour. Although they are readers, the symbols help the pupils to be sure they understand what is expected of them. Missing a crucial word could have significant effect on the outcome – 'You invite me …' is very different from 'You never invite me…' .

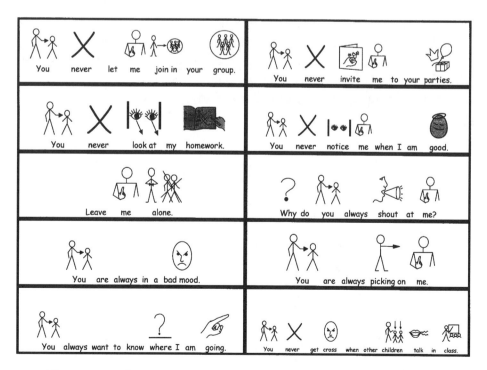

Figure 1.4 *Sentences to help students think about their feelings*

Justin Drew, a speech and language therapist in Sandwell, produces many resources for the pupils in the schools he works with. This example helps a non-speech child to participate in retelling a story. The same vocabulary can be used to re-tell the story in writing at a later stage.

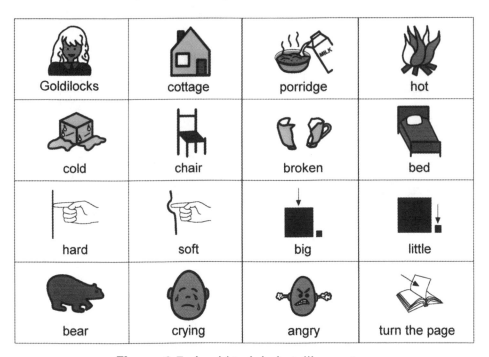

Figure 1.5 *A grid to join in telling a story*

Susan Burnes, supporting her son at home

Susan Burnes uses symbols at home with her autistic son, to help him develop literacy skills. She has devised a host of activities and games that he enjoys, from 'request' cards and labels to support his speech, to games and literacy activities. She found that the symbols formed an essential part of the process.

These same techniques are also used in many schools, as part of the literacy strategy.

Figure 1.6 *Supporting literacy*

Children in a nursery

Springfield Nursery, Witney, is an assessment unit for pre-school pupils with special educational needs. The atmosphere is one of informality, but the pupils need to have some structure within their day, and to feel safe and secure there. This is partly developed by giving the pupils a sense of time and what is happening to them. They use symbols as a means of communicating the activities that are going to happen, to reflect on what they have done, and to give a shape to the day. A symbol is linked to each activity. These symbols are pasted onto card and covered with plastic film. String loops are attached so they can be hung on hooks in a line but are easy to reach and handle. Each morning the group collect the symbols for the activities of the day and talk about what will happen. Before each activity the symbol is passed around so that every child sees it. Similarly, when an activity has finished, the card is passed around before it is replaced on its hook. There are a number of games in the room that the children can also play to familiarise themselves with the symbols.

Other examples of using symbols to represent timetable activities, are shown in Chapter 9.

Figure 1.7 *Activity cards ready to use in a nursery*

Keeping in contact

Sam is 13. He is a fortnightly boarder at a school for students with severe learning difficulties. His mother described how 'He recently wrote a letter home to me, using a word processor program assisted by symbols as well as words. I have a computer at home and feel that this software could open up a valuable and exciting new method of dialogue between my son and myself.'

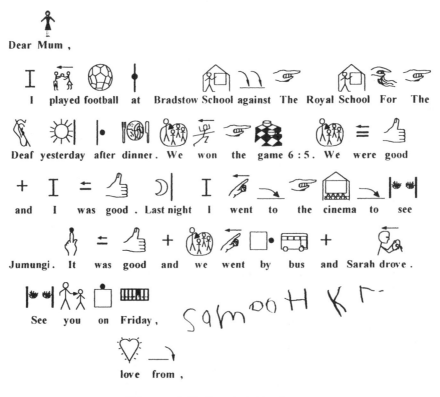

Figure 1.8 *Sam's letter home*

3. Using computers

One of the major factors in increasing the use of symbols has been computer software and programs which allow easy reproduction of symbols. Before the widespread use of computers the only way of creating symbol materials was by drawing the symbols yourself (difficult and inconsistent) or by photocopying and pasting (time-consuming). Computers and symbol software have made the process of making materials very much more accessible to both professionals or carers and users.

Writing with Symbols, designed by the authors, was originally developed with financial assistance from the Nuffield Foundation. Its aim was to allow the user to produce symbols simply by typing the symbol name. Over the years the program has been extensively developed. It can now be used with the three major symbol sets used in the UK: Rebus, Makaton and PCS (Picture Communication Symbols). Now you can write in text and symbols, or mainly in text, showing the occasional symbol, you can create grids of symbols and symbol phrases, and most importantly, users can write by directly selecting symbols from a grid. More recent extensions allow users to send and receive email, or save pages of symbols as HTML files suitable for putting on the web.

Symbols can also be individually incorporated into many other types of application, for example, into Desk Top publishing programs or making displays and interactive learning materials in presentation packages. The power of these techniques are discussed more fully later.

4. Pressures to use symbols

The reason for using symbols is not because there are easy ways of creating materials using them, but for the benefits that they can bring.

Since the 1960s there has been a steady growth in opportunities for children and young people with disabilities to have access to education. More recently, there has also been a concern to increase opportunities for adults with disabilities to participate more in society. Successive legislation in many countries has promoted this trend. A further impetus has been provided by the move towards inclusive education. Instead of providing different educational environments with different objectives and strategies, we are moving towards a system in which each person can have access to the same types of educational experiences and opportunities for participation, but within a differentiated curriculum.

Whatever the context, the most fundamental requirement for participation is communication.

> In a human being, communication difficulties are arguably the most significant deficit of all. If acute, not only do they exclude him from any major involvement in society, but they may also limit intellectual development and will certainly hinder educational progress. (Jones and Cregan 1986: 5)

For this reason, the major educational development for pupils with learning difficulties has been focused on improving communication. In UK schools this was first embedded within the context of a National Curriculum which started to recognise the importance of communication. It was supported by the Code of Practice on the Identification and Assessment of Special Educational Needs (DFE 1994) with an emphasis on encouraging student involvement in decision-making and recording achievement. The Code of Practice specifically indicated: 'Where appropriate, Records of Achievement ... can make use of pictorial or abstract symbol systems' (DFE 1994 6:54). And more recently this aim was emphasised by the Communication Aid Project, set up in 2001 and managed by BECTa (British Educational Communications and Technology agency). This initiative provides mechanisms for pupils to be assessed and, where necessary, to receive help with the purchase of essential equipment and software to support their communication needs.

Outside the field of education the UK Children Act (1989), in addition, required all children and young people to be given the opportunity to express their views about provision made for them, implicitly supporting a diversity of communication strategies. Children who have learning difficulties and who may not be able to record their views through written words or who need help to understand questions and choices, also need help to express their views, including alternative accessible means of communication, including written communication and recording.

Within the adult sector, UK legislation has stressed 'care in the community' rather than institutional care. The White Paper, *Valuing People* (Department of Health March 2001) sets out a programme of measures to increase participation and independence. This has highlighted the need for improved communication skills for those adults who have not had the benefit of a communication-focused education. These changes in structure and legislation have contributed to a very significant growth in the use of symbols with learning disabled adults. As legislation increases opportunities for people with different disabilities, the importance of communication for all becomes ever more evident.

5. A continuum of need

Until the late 1990s there was often a big divide between the discrete provision for those with special needs and pupils educated in ordinary schools with each sector adopting quite different resources and strategies. The use of symbols was seen as almost exclusively within the special schools' domain, directed in one of the two following areas, often regarded as quite distinct groups:

1. People who have severe communication difficulties who require the use of an Aided and Augmentative Communication (AAC) system.
2. Pupils with severe learning difficulties, who require prompts and cues for both communication and learning.

The use of symbols to facilitate communication for people who are unable to speak has been common practice for many years. Intellectually able non-speech people are often able to use abstract symbol systems which give access to extensive vocabularies. Other people, with cognitive difficulties, have tended to use more pictorial symbols and smaller vocabularies. In practice, of course, there are no discrete groups, but it is a continuum of need and capability.

It is beyond the scope of this book to specifically explore the role of symbols for people in the first group. In-depth discussion of this may be found in *Augmentative and Alternative Communication* (Lonke *et al.* 1999), Chapters 15–19). In contrast, *Symbols Now* (Abbott 2000) contains a very wide range of examples of symbols supporting students and adults in the second group, who have a range of learning or communication difficulties.

The developments in educational and social policy have drawn attention to the need for a variety of communication strategies for people with literacy difficulties. As attitudes to inclusivity in both schools and in society at large have developed, there has been a broadening of situations in which symbols can support communication and now we are seeing a diversity of situations where they are being used to support the acquisition of literacy. In ordinary schools symbols may provide a support or bridge to traditional orthography, or just a motivation to reluctant readers and writers. These different aspects of symbols use are discussed in more depth in later chapters. One of the philosophies behind this book is that just as there is a continuum of need, there can also be a continuum of response, and that strategies that may be used intensively for some learners can provide appropriate transition routes for others, and there are many examples where an idea can be applied to meet a wide spectrum of need.

6. Types of symbols

Different types of graphic images are used in communication. They range from pictures through to text (which can be regarded as a series of graphic elements which combine to carry meaning). Symbols are representations that lie between these two extremes. They differ from pictures because each symbol represents a single concept, whereas a picture may portray a complex of ideas.

Symbol images range between those which are rather like simplified pictures, through to abstract images which can be combined to form syntactical units.

Non-pictorial systems

Blissymbolics
Blissymbolics is different from all of the other symbol sets in that it most resembles a written language. It is a 'nonphonetic and meaning based system' (Schlosser 1997) and is created from nine basic shapes to represent 3,500 vocabulary items. Although the Blissymbol system appears to be highly abstract, it is inherently logical as each component represents a single concept.

The basic building block within the Blissymbolic language is the Bliss-character. Each Bliss-character represents a concrete or abstract meaning. The Blissymbolic Character Set is the collection of all Bliss-characters which make up the Blissymbolic language. Bliss-characters can be set in sequence to form new meanings. A sequence of one or more Bliss-characters is referred to as a Bliss-word. Each Bliss-word carries a gloss which corresponds to its spoken language translation. The structure of the system enables the user to expand a small number of basic characters into a vocabulary of infinite size. Bliss-characters may be combined to create new symbol expressions.

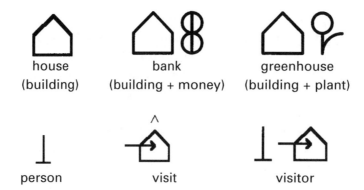

house	bank	greenhouse
(building)	(building + money)	(building + plant)

person	visit	visitor

The meanings of each Bliss-word is dependent on the size, orientation and position of the basic shapes. 'Special characters' enable users to create novel words and utterances without substantially adding to the total number of items in a user's communication system. e.g. an action indicator added to nouns creates verbs.

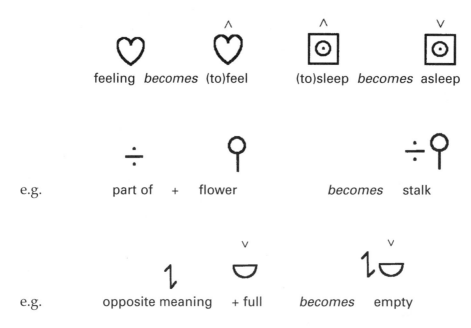

feeling *becomes* (to)feel   (to)sleep *becomes* asleep

e.g.   part of   +   flower   *becomes*   stalk

e.g.   opposite meaning   + full   *becomes*   empty

Above all, Blissymbol communication provides the user with the ability to communicate in sentences.

The flexibility of this type of symbol makes it function in a similar way to other written languages. However, they do not rely on matching salient visual features, but relate to the referent via the phonological or semantic domains (Schlosser 1996), and for this reason may not always be the most appropriate images for people with learning difficulties.

Bliss symbols were originally developed as an international language to help conflict resolution. They were later introduced as a language to non-speaking, physically disabled children and adults. They are visually and cognitively more demanding than more pictorial images which makes them less suitable for users who have learning difficulties. (Symbol Users Advisory Group 1994)

Pictorial symbols

Pictorial symbols tend to be representational and are used more widely with children and adults with learning disabilities. Richle *et al.* (1991) drew attention to studies which indicated that some learners with severe learning disabilities were more able to associate meaning with simple iconic line drawings than with full colour pictures. They also point out that such iconic symbols were more easily acquired, generalised and maintained by users with severe learning difficulties than the more abstract Blissymbolics. More abstract ideas, however, may need more abstract symbols even within a pictorial symbol system and this is discussed more fully in Chapter 2.

The first use of pictorial symbols as an aid to literacy was devised for the Peabody Rebus Reading Program whose authors were based at the George Peabody College, Tennessee in the 1960s (Jones and Cregan 1986). This was originally developed as part of a reading scheme to help young disadvantaged children, and those with learning difficulties, to develop the sub-skills required for traditional orthography, i.e. reading and writing with standard text. The types of symbols varied between those that were pictorial – representing pictures; ideographic – representing ideas in relatively concrete form; and symbols which tended to be more arbitrary or abstract in design.

Rebus symbols
In the UK the Rebus approach was adopted and developed in the late 1970s and early 1980s. The most significant of these initiatives was at Rees Thomas School, in Cambridgeshire, and was developed by Judy van Oosterom and Kathleen Devereux. Starting in 1974 and working with pupils with a range of learning difficulties, Judy van Oosterom explored ways in which this pictorial approach could enhance the development of language and concepts. *Learning with Rebuses* (Devereux and van Oosterom 1984) describes their approach and the methods employed. It was clear from their reports that the use of pictorial or representational symbols could be very beneficial to learning. Judy pioneered strategies for using symbols to enhance literacy and understanding of language, and was initially quite independent of initiatives developing symbols that supported face-to-face aided communication.

In her work, van Oosterom redesigned many of the original Peabody Rebus symbols as well as adding to the vocabulary. The original Rebus approach also used homonyms (similar sounding words). For example, a picture of the insect 'bee' would be used to indicate the verb in 'to be'. This use of symbols, described by Friscoe and Lloyd (1979, cited in Jones and Cregan 1986) as 'semantically aberrant', was one of the first aspects that van Oosterom addressed by redesigning the abstract symbols that these represented. The use of homonyms is no longer considered acceptable.

Other pictorial symbol systems were developed at about the same time. The main ones are mentioned below. Gillian Hazell, from the ACE Centre, Oxford, has compiled more detailed information, on which the following is based.

The **Rebus** Symbol Collection has largely been developed through project work with schools, colleges and adult communities. Although it is a pictorial symbol set, it has an underlying schematic structure which has been considerably strengthened in the recent major redevelopment, which is described in the next chapter.

karaoke   this   fun   gorilla   therapist

The Makaton Vocabulary Development Project (MVDP)
This was initially developed to provide a functional signing system for people with learning disabilities, and later, initially through links with Rebus, developed symbols to complement the signs. The Makaton symbol set contains a number of grammatical elements, often using letters with visual indicators.

HARBOUR   SEASONS   MAGNET   DEPTH   TO BALANCE
from Geography Features   from Geography (Time)   from Science   from Maths   from P.E.

There is a core of some hundreds of symbols that are essentially common to both Makaton and Rebus symbols, although the drawing styles have diverged. Beyond that base, symbol development has continued independently, although many of the conventions and structures are very similar. This positive feature of the two systems suggests that they can easily be used to complement each other to build wider vocabularies, although they have different approaches to parts of speech and grammatical markers. Both systems have been extensively developed in recent years and comprise very substantial vocabularies for social and educational purposes.

Picture Communication Symbols (PCS) from Mayer-Johnson (US)
Picture Communication Symbols, developed in the United States, have also grown out of the original Rebus developments in Nashville. Many of the symbols are similar to those in the Rebus and Makaton collections, while others are more pictorial than the UK equivalents. A particular strength of this system is the extensive range of social symbols suitable across a wide age range. These symbols are also commonly used in the UK, adding to the range of alternatives. One particular difference is that the PCS symbols are available in colour, which is very motivating to many users, especially people in the earlier stages of symbol communication.

laugh   meeting   queue   problem   bank clerk

Compics
Compic symbols were developed in Australia. Most Compics are easy to understand, although there are no representations of abstract vocabulary.

I need .. I agree disagree go / went home

PIC (Pictogram, Ideogram Communication)

PIC symbols, which were developed in Sweden, are very representational symbols. There are few abstract symbols, making the set more suitable for users with more severe cognitive difficulties. One of the chief differences is that they appear white on black.

Sigsymbols (UK)

Sigsymbols were originally devised as a bridge between signing and symbols. This was the first system to be designed particularly to address the needs of pupils with severe learning difficulties. These symbols were concerned with direct communication and eliciting spoken or signed language. Significantly, Cregan (1982) encouraged users to develop new symbols according to defined criteria as they were needed. This aspect was considered important. The intention was to present opportunities for vocabulary development as in Bliss symbols, moving it towards a 'living language'.

Jump   lady   like   look   many

The systems described above by no means comprise an exhaustive list and each system available has both advantages and disadvantages. This book aims to discuss the educational and social purposes of symbols rather than recommend any one symbol system because:

> comparative studies of different symbol systems generally argue in favour of using symbols that are most guessable. However, every user has a unique personal history that may override this general principle … It is imperative, therefore, to determine the most appropriate symbol system for each learner individually. (Richle *et al.* 1991:49)

It is arguable, therefore, that individual symbols chosen for particular purposes or individuals could be drawn from any of these systems if that were appropriate. Such a pragmatic approach to symbol use has both advantages and disadvantages, and the consequent implications of this are discussed in later chapters.

Whichever particular system is used, there are certain common features, and the issues of teaching and learning remain the same. The authors have been closely associated with the development of Rebus symbols and so there will inevitably be more examples given using that particular symbol set. The principles, however, apply to all pictorial sets and we feel that those who use other systems will have no difficulty in applying the ideas to their own system.

Summary

To set the scene, the chapter opened with illustrations of some people who have found symbols of value and some of the pressures which lie behind a recent growth in symbol use. The particular factors which have been identified are the social and legislative pressures for increased access to education, information and participation and the advent of computers and symbol-processing software, which have helped to make the use of symbols very much easier. After describing the context for symbol use, the chapter gave a brief history of the use of symbols to support pupils and students who have difficulties with text, and went on to describe a few of the common symbol sets currently in use. The next chapter looks at the nature of symbols and in particular describes the structure of the new Rebus symbols, and finally discusses the relationship between the graphic image and the text it supports.

2 Principles of pictorial symbols

This chapter discusses the main principles of pictorial symbols. It considers the nature of symbols, some issues of symbols design, illustrated through the re-development of the new Widgit Rebus set. It then begins to look at some of the graphical/linguistic issues raised by using symbols.

1. Pictures, illustrations and symbols

Before discussing the nature of symbols, it may be useful to consider the nature of the images that may be used in a communication system. These range from photographs or very detailed pictures, to simplified pictures or illustrations through to symbols. We saw in the previous chapter that even within the range of symbols that there is considerable variety.

Pictures

Figure 2.1 *A complex photograph*

Figure 2.2 *A simple picture with a single concept*

Figure 2.1 on its own could be illustrating one of several ideas: It could be 'Mike', the person in the photograph, it could be representing a library or the idea of work or of 'Mike working'. Without a caption it is not possible to know which of these is the intention. On the other hand, Figure 2.2 clearly represents a single person. The photograph will be much clearer than any other kind of illustration or drawing, and may be the most appropriate way to represent that person in any system.

There are some images that cannot be adequately represented in symbol form, for example, individual people or special places. By including photographs with symbols the material can be made more communicative. The Park School in Buckinghamshire has photographs of all the pupils, so that when they write with symbols, each pupil's or teacher's name is represented by their photograph. The Park School in Sheffield, on the other hand, has made stationery for each student which includes their photograph. This means that the ownership of every piece of work is clear, and non-readers can hand out and collect in the group's work without needing to read names.

Illustrations

An illustration is a simplified drawing. It is likely to show a complexity of ideas rather than a single concept.

Figure 2.3 *Illustrations and clip art*

The illustration on the left may be quite confusing unless you know what it is about. It could be attack, strangle or many things. The caption would show that it is illustrating the Heimlich manoeuvre, and the illustration supported by some text will give a much clearer indication of the action than any text description alone. The illustration, therefore, supports a larger idea rather than a single word/concept. The illustration on the right, of Henry VIII, on the other hand, is more like the example of the girl's photograph. There was only one Henry VIII and it is inappropriate to create a generic symbolic representation for this specific character.

Today we see symbols in many environments, such as road signs, labelling, and on computers. Many of these symbols are used internationally to overcome language barriers while others are used by specific disciplines or communities for more particular purposes.

Figure 2.4 *Some common symbols*

Some of these symbols are pictorial and easily communicate their meaning, others are more abstract and need to be learned. Their pictorial nature, however, makes them easily recognised and remembered. These do not, however, form part of a substantial set and may be more helpfully regarded as illustrations or clip-art.

Symbols

The principle of having recognisable representations of objects, actions or attributes makes the use of symbols of interest as a means of communication for people with literacy and learning difficulties. The great advantage of pictorial symbols over more abstract symbol systems is that they can more easily be understood, whatever the age, language or reading ability of the reader.

For most people who are able to read, the use of symbols is concerned with communicating ideas very quickly and simply. For people with severe learning disabilities, they may provide the *only* means whereby meaning can be communicated in printed form. Take the following example:

Поставтье дверь на замок

Выключите свет!

Figure 2.5 *Symbols can convey meaning when the text does not*

For those of us who cannot read Russian it is impossible to find the meaning from the text alone. The presence of the symbols, while not providing a direct translation of the text, gives clues to its meaning. The first phrase certainly has something to do with locks and doors, and the other concerns switches and lights. The symbols provide a clue to the meaning which provides a considerable advantage over the otherwise incomprehensible text. If the notice is explained first, the reader is likely to find it easier to recall the meaning from the symbols than from the unfamiliar letters.

What a symbol communicates may vary from one situation to another. In a personal communication book a mixture of photographs, drawings and symbols may be used to represent specific people, and situations as well as general concepts. The individual user will negotiate and learn the particular meanings in this instance. In this case these symbols may stand for quite complex or contextual information:

let's go to another shop   how do you play   point to symbols   show

Figure 2.6 *Symbols used on a communication board*

The PCS collection, which was designed to support aided communication, is particularly suited to this type of use. In these cases the images may not communicate the precise meaning, but rather remind the communicators of a meaning already agreed.

Many symbol users, working with communication books or communication aids, use a range of somewhat personalised vocabulary to facilitate their direct communication. In written communication the meaning needs to become more specific, as there is a closer link between the images and the exact meaning. A symbol will represent a single concept rather than a whole idea. This requires a much closer relationship between text or spoken language and its graphical representation. At this level, at least the main information-carrying words will each have a symbol, and at the most complex level there may be symbols associated with each word used.

2. Understanding symbols

Not all meanings can be represented by images that are immediately recognisable. As the nature of the idea becomes more abstract or more complex, so the nature of the symbol changes. Across the range of vocabulary there will be symbols whose meaning needs to be learned. Just as words need to be taught to children learning to read, many symbols must also be taught. While some symbols may be easily recognisable, it is not realistic to put a page of symbols in front of a reader and expect him or her to understand it exactly.

It is helpful to think of pictorial symbols falling into four classes which need varying degrees of teaching.

Group 1. Transparent or guessable symbols

These pictorial symbols are usually recognisable and need little teaching.

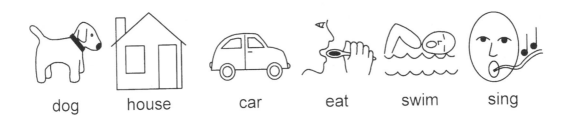

dog   house   car   eat   swim   sing

Group 2. Translucent or learnable symbols

These symbols often fall into groups or schema, which can help their 'learnability'.

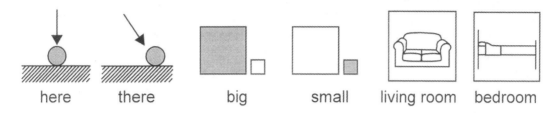

In some cases the very pictorial nature of the symbol can help to communicate the concepts within the group. For example, the pictorial nature of 'in' and 'on' or 'this' and 'that' may help the student to more clearly distinguish between the ideas.

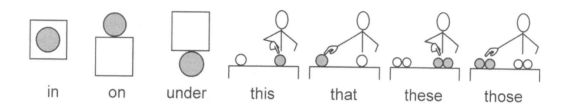

Once the concept of the group has been understood, it is not necessary to learn every example. Explaining related symbols in groups will help students see the meaning of the symbol more clearly, and they will be more likely to recognise other symbols in the group when they see them. This makes a good strategy for teaching, and when a symbol that falls into such a group is first seen, it is worthwhile taking time out to illustrate the related symbols.

Group 3. Opaque or symbols which need to be learned

As the vocabulary and ideas become more complex, so does the representational nature of the symbols used to represent them. All symbols representing more abstract concepts will need explanation, but a person with a learning disability may have a much better chance of recalling the meaning with the help of the graphic image than through an unrecognisable text alternative. Such symbols include concepts like:

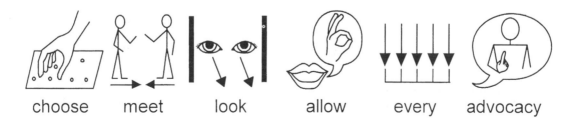

These symbols are created from elements connected with the idea, but the reader will require some explanation of the way in which the image relates to the meaning.

There is plenty of anecdotal evidence that suggests that users who are familiar with symbols can understand quite complex representations. In a training session carers were discussing the symbol for 'independent'. During the conversation Kate, an adult with a learning disability, was asked whether she thought this symbol was acceptable, and in particular whether it mattered that the people crossed out were smaller. She was quite adamant that it was better for them to be small. Pointing to the larger 'me' part of the symbol she said, 'This is like me coming on my own on the bus', which is what she had done that morning and was really proud of. However, she went on to say that what she wanted was a lot of people crossed out, as if to establish her independence of the whole world.

It is sometimes suggested that a person who is able to understand some of these complex concepts will have the skills necessary to be able to read. This is not supported by current evidence. Experience tells us that there are many people who cannot read but who can both understand and use the concepts together with the symbols related to them.

Group 4. Symbols which are purely abstract

These are symbols which cannot be illustrated. This is the most difficult group of symbols, as the user has not only to learn the meaning, but also their use in sentence construction.

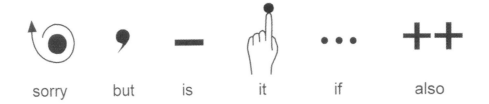

| sorry | but | is | it | if | also |

The design of these symbols is somewhat arbitrary. Some of the abstract symbols have come from signs, such as 'sorry'.

Abstract symbols need to be taught and learned. Their use will depend on the individual reader. Some readers will be able to learn the text for small words such as 'it' and 'is'. Other readers may find the graphics easier to distinguish than the text and the addition of a symbol can help draw their attention to the finer differences of the text. One teacher reported that using symbols when a child gets stuck with 'is', 'it' 'if' and 'in' considerably shortens the time taken to overcome this particular hurdle.

Fortunately a great deal of meaning can be conveyed without using many of these abstract symbols, or in some cases, any at all. Young children, at the beginning of language development, will often read from the key information-carrying pictures and then infer the additional words. In other contexts alternative, simpler phrases which do not need these more abstract symbols may be more appropriate. This is discussed more fully in Chapter 7.

3. Choosing images that are appropriate to the user's understanding

It is important to use symbols within the level of understanding of the user. Many symbol users will confine themselves to levels 1 and possibly 2 from the above list, and may even use a mixture of pictures and symbols. As the cognitive level increases or the user becomes more familiar with reading symbols, higher levels of symbols may be introduced. However, whatever level of symbols are used, it is a prerequisite that the reader understands the concept of the word, just as it is in understanding text. Symbols cannot of themselves teach the meaning, but only serve as a reminder of a concept that is already understood.

At the most basic levels there is little difference in essence between transparent symbols of one set to another.

Figure 2.7 *The same concept in PCS, Rebus, and Makaton symbols*

At level 1 (guessable), there is little difference between the sets, other than stylistic variation. As the level of the symbols change, the differences between the sets become greater. Symbols in groups 3 and 4 can vary quite significantly between the sets.

4. Symbol systems and symbol sets

Collections of symbols have been divided into two categories: (a) symbol sets, which have a fixed content, although the design of the symbols, while obeying conventions, does not fundamentally have rules; and (b) symbol systems which have a clearly defined structure and set of rules by which the vocabulary can be extended (Schlosser 1997).

Blissymbolics is the only symbol collection that is truly systematic. However, the pictorial symbol sets that have developed from the US Rebuses have tended to adopt a more schematic approach for at least parts of their vocabulary. They have identified certain conventions to provide additional qualifications to the meaning of the basic symbol. Many of these conventions are shared, having evolved from the same roots and been developed in similar environments.

Figure 2.8 Similar conventions used in different symbol sets

Like the representational symbols which fall into groups, once the convention has been understood, the user does not have to learn every incidence of it.

Other conventions such as indicating tenses have similarities but are not identical. At a higher language level the use of grammatical markers makes significant differences between the symbol sets.

5. Extending and developing vocabularies

The initial small vocabularies of the early symbol sets were fine for communication books, labelling and very basic pictorial representation. The expansion in symbol use has demanded a significant extension to the vocabularies available. The Rebus, Makaton and PCS symbol sets, in particular, have done a great deal of development work. Each of them has also consolidated its style and structure. This section will look at the structure of the Rebus Symbol Collection and its recent development, in order to illustrate the direction in which pictorial symbols are moving and demonstrate the potential for literacy support.

The New Widgit Rebus symbols

The initial schema of the Rebus Symbol Collection was published in 1992 in the *Rebus Glossary* (van Oosterom and Devereux 1992). However, over the following eight years the sets had been contributed to by many practitioners and some of the initial schema needed to be reviewed. In the interests of speed and meeting rapid demands, not all the new symbols had been devised within a strict style.

Between October 2000 and the summer of 2002 a major revision of this symbol set was undertaken in the light of changing demands of symbol users. As well as strengthening the presentation there was a strong desire to make the set more systematic, so that there would be rules or conventions that would allow a measure of vocabulary extension. The idea was to create a symbol set that would be mainly pictographic but with a systematic approach, placing itself mid-way between the systematic form of Blissymbolics and the more illustrative images of PCS. Such an addition to the range of symbols available might be helpful in supporting the continuum of need described earlier.

Some of the revised conventions are described below.

Personalisation

A circle around an item indicates a special relationship.

Buildings and shops

Buildings and shops use a generic form containing a specific symbol showing the function.

Large buildings and shops

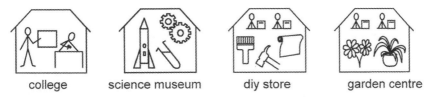

An alternative 'large building' element has been added to distinguish between buildings such as clinic and hospital, or corner shop and supermarket.

Days, and dates

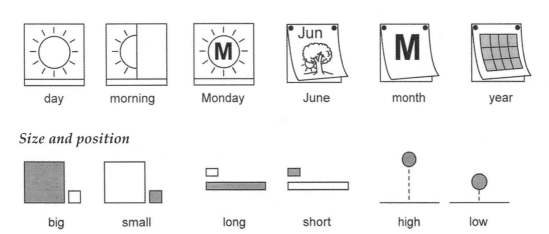

Size and position

Generally, size and position require a visual comparison. The new convention is to identify the target item through shading. The earlier version used indicating arrows. However, these arrows were generally not noticed or understood. Arrows are used much more selectively, to indicate direction or movement.

Pronouns

| I | my | you | your | we | our |

Pronouns such as I, you, he, and indicative pronouns (me, you, him) are represented by a pointing hand. Possessive pronouns (her, hers) are represented by a small black circle (for clenched fist).

Collectives and groups

| animals | group | science | committee | music |

These tend to be represented by a small group of characteristic items. Where it forms a specific group, such as in a school subject, then grouping brackets are added.

Negatives

| don't like | haven't | nobody | Don't | touch | no | milk |

Some common negatives are shown with a strong red or grey line through. Alternatively, either the symbol for 'No' or 'Not' is used as appropriate.

Emphasis

| great | awful | work hard |

An exclamation mark is widely understood as giving emphasis.

Plurals

| cars | fish | teachers | books |

Many symbol users do not understand the idea of plurals, and it has been common practice to use the single image for both singular and plural nouns. At the higher levels of language, it may be important to discriminate, in which case a plural qualifier is added.

A small vocabulary with multiple images is also given to help introduce the concept of plurals, but obviously this will only be suitable for concepts that are graphically simple.

Tenses

| I | ate | We | ran | You | will | swim |

Simple past tense uses a back arrow, and in English, the future tense is invariably made with the word 'will' which is the symbol for 'is' with the forward arrow.

There are occasions when symbol users who are working at higher language levels want to use more complex past tenses – such as 'I have eaten' or 'I was running'. In the earlier version of Rebus the only representation for the verb 'have' was the possessive image (a hand holding something). This was conceptually wrong for the past tense, and so an alternative has been devised indicating 'time past'.

| I | have | eaten | I | was | eating |

Questions

| when | where | what |

When these words are used as questions, a question mark is added to the graphic.

Clearly, these examples do not cover the entire vocabulary or grammatical range. However, it outlines the thinking behind the symbol set. It is hoped that this revised symbol set will sit comfortably with the more pictorial PCS symbol set, offering the option to develop and extend symbol use in areas of literacy.

It is the hope of the authors that symbols will be developed that transcend international barriers. Spoken languages and sign languages restrict international communication, and it is hoped that by designing a symbol system that is not based on word sounds and does not include text elements, we will create a tool for greater communication. This does not, of course, preclude a localised symbol vocabulary where appropriate.

6. Alternative symbols

One of the most important issues in written symbols is ensuring that the right graphic is chosen for the concept.

At a simple level it is providing different images for words with the same spelling: for example, 'I want a **drink**' and 'I will **drink** some coffee'.

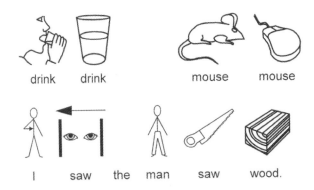

drink	drink		mouse		mouse

| I | saw | the | man | saw | wood. |

There are other words which have meanings which are even less related. For example, the animal 'mouse' and a computer 'mouse', the game 'draughts' and a 'draught' of air, to give just two examples. Selection of the appropriate image is very important in these situations if the meaning is to make sense at all.

A particularly difficult set of vocabulary are the words 'do', 'make' and 'work'. As well as standing for a single concept on their own, they can also be used to augment or modify meaning. For example the word 'do' has three types of use:

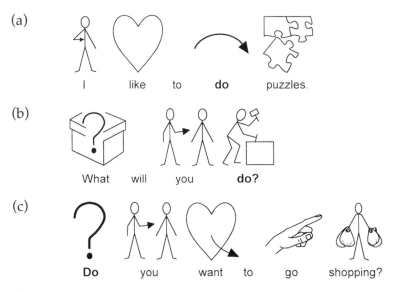

(a) I like to **do** puzzles.

(b) What will you **do?**

(c) **Do** you want to go shopping?

(a) is an emphatic use of 'do', using an alternative for 'work'.
(b) uses 'do' as an incidental verb and so uses a generic 'action' element.
(c) is not really about action. The 'do' converts the sentence into a question.
 'Work' similarly has different meanings, and therefore different symbols:

7. Symbols and text

Although symbols are normally displayed with the associated text, not all text may be supported by a symbol. The relationship between the symbol and the text will depend upon the reader's cognitive level and the reason that they are using symbols. It may be helpful to think of two types of symbol use: one where the symbols are the main communicative items, the other is where the symbols are being used as a support or bridge towards traditional orthography.

Symbols as the principal means of communication

At this level the symbols are the principal line of communication rather than any printed text. The text is included for a carer or non-symbol reader, and also possibly to help the reader learn to recognise some text.

 The sequence and the choice of vocabulary will help to convey meaning in the simplest way. The purpose is to gain meaning directly from the symbols.

Symbols as a support for text

At this level the purpose is to assist the reader towards an exact reading of the written words.

(a) Symbols may be used with every word:

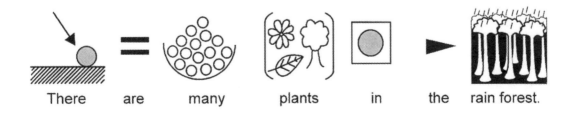

(b) or symbols will only be used with those words that require support:

Use   a sharp knife to chop the onion.

    In both of these examples the symbols are not seen as part of an integrated linguistic structure in themselves, instead, the structure is determined by the spoken or written text. It may not be necessary to attach a symbol to every word of the text, but to provide support for words that cannot be read. The symbols are not seen as a complete communication in themselves, but as separate elements supporting individual words.

    Where the base text is simple, this approach will work for many different users. As the text becomes more complex, the second approach is more tenable.

Summary

This chapter has considered different types of images, including symbols. It has looked at different levels of symbol images and at some of the conventions of symbol design. It then touched on the relationship between symbols and text. This theme is picked up elsewhere in the book as are essential differences in symbols being used to support receptive and expressive communication.

3 Starting to use symbols

This chapter gives examples and ideas of many ways in which symbols can be introduced to new users. The chapter is essentially very practical, and aims to provoke thought about how symbols can contribute in a range of circumstances and across the phases of education and life, and to support both receptive and expressive communication. The examples are drawn from practice, but can be modified for other users in different contexts. Many of the games devised for children could easily be adapted for older users, and some of the strategies used with adults could have relevance for younger users. Four approaches are described: symbols in the environment, symbols supporting face-to-face communication, games involving symbols and exploring symbols through writing.

1. Symbols in the environment

Most children learn to read their first words by seeing them in the environment, on food packets, toys, etc. If symbol readers are to gain the same level of familiarity with this different medium, those also should be seen in their surroundings. The example shown in Chapter 1, at Springfield Nursery, shows how this familiarity helped the children to relate meaning to image. The pupils also used a computer program to look at the symbols in their vocabulary. Exploring new knowledge or ideas through a variety of different activities and media can provide valuable language reinforcement.

It is now quite usual when entering a special school to see displays labelled with symbols all over the school. For example, all the displays at Wilson Stuart School in Birmingham have symbol captions. In the nursery all notices are supported by both symbols and objects of reference for familiarisation as well as information, and in the rest of the primary department all cupboards and storage boxes are labelled so that pupils see the symbols and text together as normal.

Adult centres too are starting to identify key places and items with symbol labels. These also help to raise the general awareness of symbols with the users and the community. Labels have been used for many years at Borehamwood Day Centre both to introduce symbols and to aid memory. One member of the Centre was very upset that everybody put the crockery away in the wrong cupboards. To solve this problem they decided to label the cupboards. The group went to a lot of trouble to agree to the most appropriate symbols for each cupboard. The aim was that by seeing these symbols regularly, each person would gradually learn to recognise the right cupboard for each item.

We are used to seeing icons or symbols guiding us around airports, shopping centres and other public places. It must be very frustrating studying or working in an environment where all the information is unreadable.

2. Supporting communication

We have already explained that it is beyond the scope of this book to discuss the depth of symbol use in formal AAC systems, but this book would be incomplete without a brief discussion of this topic.

One area that is attracting quite a lot of interest is in the structured uses of symbols to facilitate interaction for pupils on the autistic spectrum. The TEAACH approach encourages the use of visual aids to help people with autism to make sense of the world. Symbols are closely positioned to the objects or actions they represent, gradually the symbol is moved away from the object until it becomes portable, and able to be used away from the referent.

A specific structured implementation of this approach is offered by the Picture Exchange System (PECS). There are six phases in which the child learns to extend a direct concrete exchange through to constructing simple sentences both as requests and comments. Penny Fry from Salterns School in Hampshire has been using PECs for about three years, she says: 'I have found it helps pupils from those with PMLD right through to those who just need a little help to stay focused … and [I] just continue to find more ways that it benefits the pupils.'

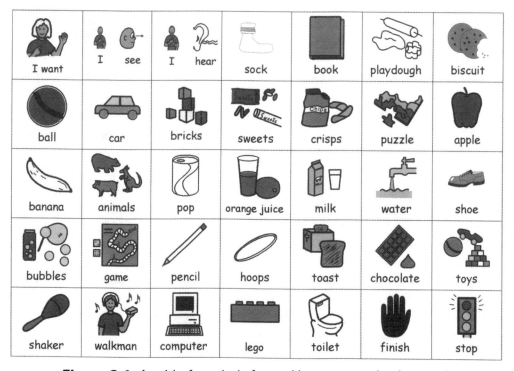

Figure 3.1 *A grid of symbols for making communication cards*

This communication sheet was created by Speech and Language Therapist Justin Drew, to facilitate communication of PECs users in a nursery classroom. Children who are more able to make the link between symbol and referent may use simple communication books or charts, both for immediate requests, or to facilitate participation in group activities. An interesting approach by Patti King-de Baun (from the USA), includes stories about and for children with disabilities. These stories are supported by symbols and each one has a communication grid ready-made to help the child re-telling it. Although there are, to date, no equivalent published stories, teachers are creating these grids themselves to facilitate participation.

Context-related aids may help young people who find it difficult to communicate in new situations. Ann McDonald from Faversham Social Education Centre created symbol labels as tags which are put onto key rings. The student takes a key ring with several symbols relating to a particular context – such as going to lunch at college. These symbols are produced to help communication when difficulties arise. The student will find the appropriate symbol and show it to explain the word or phrase that is not being understood. Clatterbridge School, Wirral, devised a similar system using a Filofax. Pages of about six symbols were put together in topic groups. It was used by students travelling on the bus, in shops and for other local activities. Others have used credit card holders in a similar fashion. The Filofax, as with the key ring, is a socially acceptable device, making the students feel more willing to use this aid.

Reinforcing meaning

It is important to make sure that any communication is understood in the same way by everybody. Using symbols can help achieve that common understanding. A person communicating in ways which are not always accurately understood, such as eye-pointing, or unclear speech, can become discouraged.

Margarida Nunes da Ponte (1996), working in Portugal with pupils who have severe communication difficulties, has some very positive ways of increasing the confidence of the pupils in her class. A particularly useful symbol support, suggested by Goosens, Crain and Elder (1992), is the communication vest, sometimes called the bib-overlay. It is made of Velcro-sensitive material onto which symbol cards can easily be stuck. This facilitates expressive communication by the non-speaking child or aids language stimulation by the facilitator. It acts as a portable communication board enabling Margarida to confirm what the child selects or indicates. The symbols are moved to a blank part of the vest and thus build up a meaningful symbol sequence. Alternatively, Margarida can confirm her own speech to the child by selecting the symbols in a similar way.

Another support is the Enlarged Communication Board. This is a large board on one of the classroom walls. Large symbols are placed on the board according to semi-grammatical categories (social, people, verbs/actions, nouns, descriptive words and a 'various' group). This board can be seen from any point in the classroom and can be used either by adults pointing to symbols as they speak as aided language stimulation, or by the pupils as direct selection such as eye gazing, light pointing.

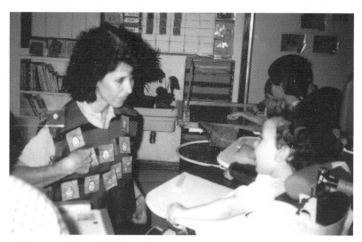

Figure 3.2 *Margarida using a 'communication vest'*

These individual examples are ones that many teachers are using. The particular feature of Margarida's approach is the open access to choices, extension of vocabulary, and clear, positive reinforcement of each communication.

Learning in context

Clearly we are all more likely to learn or remember when the content has relevance to our lives. Using symbols in timetables and daily routines can give shape to a person's day. There are many examples of timetables made with symbol cards. For example, one teacher in Surrey uses symbol cards for all the daily activities. The cards have Velcro on the back. Each morning, in circle time, the timetable for each child is built up on the wall. Their name and photograph are put at the top of the column, and the symbols for the activities are placed underneath. When each activity is completed the child can remove the symbol and put it in the 'done' bag at the bottom of the board. This helps them to get a sense of the passing of time. The same teacher supports her reinforcement with feedback cards. She has cards with individual photographs, and cards with 'remarks'. When she wants to comment, she will hold up the photograph and the card with 'Well done', etc. or 'Be quiet'.

The teacher reports that for one child with behaviour difficulties this reinforcement appears to have had particular benefits, perhaps by helping him to understand the day's progress more easily. The set of cards with each pupil's photograph, and the symbols for 'Well done', 'Be quiet', etc., can quickly be used to reinforce the communication, helping to build confidence in the situation.

3. Games to introduce symbols

The rate at which symbols become associated with the objects, actions or attributes they represent will depend upon the learner. Before associating symbols with actions and objects, a potential symbol user will need to learn to discriminate between pictures or symbols. However, this is a process of exploration and association rather than a formal learning situation and probably one of the best ways of introducing symbols is through games.

At a day centre in Somerset, the members first started by learning symbols associated with food, and using the centre's canteen. As well as using symbol cards to match with the food items, they devised all sorts of games simply to increase the time spent using and handling these images. They used games like dominoes and bingo.

Symbols are generally supported by the text to aid association for the learner as well as ensuring that any helper knows the exact meaning associated with a particular image in that context.

The games below describe activities devised by teachers. Many of them can be adapted to suit learners of different ages.

• **Snap and matching games** are easy to design. Cards can be made very quickly if the class has a computer and printer. Examples of matching games include picture to symbol, symbol to initial letter, bingo type matching, concept matching through to sorting games

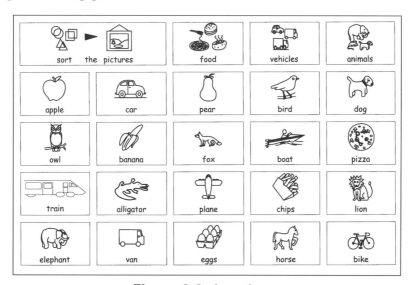

Figure 3.3 *A sorting game*

This activity, devised by Chris Hopkins, can either be stuck onto card and cut up or the student can sort by colouring.

• **Memory**: A teacher in one nursery used symbol cards to help some children to develop memory skills in a simplified version of Kim's game. A table with several objects placed on it provided the focus for this game. When the pupils had had time to observe its contents an object would be removed. A symbol card was left in its place as a clue for the pupils who found the game too hard. They then had to search around the room to find the missing object and replace it.
• **Dressing up**: this game has a symbol card for each item of clothing in the dressing up box. All the cards were laid out in a long line. Each child threw a dice in turn and stepped along the line to find their card which told them what they had to put on next. This provided a lot of fun, and was a good exercise in recognition, matching and counting.

Trish Davidson from the advisory centre CENMAC and Sally Payne from Shelly School, both in London, have gathered a number of games to support language acquisition and interaction. They found that it is useful to have games which randomly select symbols to which pupils respond.

- **Fishing**: for wheelchair users random selection can be difficult and they have designed a fishing game where the fish can be 'caught'. Each fish shape used in the game has a symbol on the back. The pupils have to say what the symbol means.
- **Dice game**: different symbols are put on each face of a large dice. After rolling the dice pupils act out the emotions or do the action shown. The literacy summer school made a fantastic monster, using a number dice and cards with 'body parts' to choose how many heads, legs, etc. the monster should have.
- **Matching with objects**: each pupil picks a symbol card for an object and then has to look through a box or bag to find the match.
- **Guessing**: clues such as 'I fly in the sky' are given about an object or action. There was a display where the symbol answers were grouped into categories. A giant paper flower on the classroom wall served as the background, and each petal of the flower was assigned to a category of words such as transport, food, animals, school. Behind each petal were lots of symbols from that category. To answer the clue the pupil first had to find the category, then the individual symbol. There is often no single correct answer, for example, 'I fly in the sky' could be solved by going to the 'animals' petal and then selecting 'bird', or by going to the 'people' petal and then selecting 'Superman'.

Judy van Oosterom devised a set of activities for three- to five-year-olds at home or in playgroups. She used symbols as a tool for exploring many language tasks. A feature of these games is progression. The lotto boards start with simple object matching, where the symbol is matched with an identical one. At the next level the task is to match collectives, so that 'animal' may be correctly matched by 'elephant' or 'cow', 'clothes' by 'trousers' or 'dress'. This higher level task is for players who can classify objects into sets and who can accept that there is more than one answer.

Action cards are similar. A child selects a card from a face-down pile on the table, or from out of a bag, and then has to respond, following the instruction on the card. Carol Allen, used this approach to help children develop ideas in creative writing. In a kind of consequences game, she used two large dice. One had pictures of children on each face, and actions on another. The participant had to roll a person dice and then an action dice to get the next sentence.

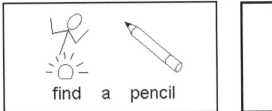 

Figure 3.4 *Action cards to stimulate comprehension, and to encourage conversation*

4. Learning through writing

Carol Allen's idea, described above, engages the user because there is an immediate and direct consequence of the selection. Constructing the meaning yourself, rather than responding to somebody else's ideas, can be more motivating to some users, especially older people. In the same way that, by writing his letter, Alan (see Figure 1.2) developed a greater engagement with the meaning, other adults start using symbols by writing about their own lives and aspirations.

As part of the Rowntree Symbols Project, Sally Paveley worked in Borehamwood Day Centre for adults with a learning disability. This project set out to explore the issues of introducing symbols to adults who had not seen them before, and to find out the most effective ways of implementation.

Reg, who attended the Centre in Borehamwood, wanted to write a piece for the Centre newsletter, but could not read, write or use symbols. Sally sat with him while he told his story and she typed it into the computer using Writing with Symbols. As she typed, a symbol appeared for each word, which they discussed. If Reg was happy with the symbol and said that he understood it, then that symbol was left in place. The others were removed. This shows just part of the final story:

Figure 3.5 *Reg's first piece of writing*

At the next meeting Sally and Reg read the story back together. Sally read the text and paused at each symbol for Reg to put those words in. As time went on Reg decided to add another symbol or two, so that he could read more of the document on his own. At the final editorial meeting each member of the group was asked to read their contribution to the newspaper. When it came to Reg's turn, someone piped up that Reg couldn't read. Undeterred, Reg produced his symbol document and read it accurately from start to finish. He was probably using a mixture of memory, symbol cues and symbol reading to speak his story, but whatever strategy he was adopting, it had enabled him to contribute and to gain a lot of self-esteem. Reg went on to increase his ability to read and write stories and information. A year later he was able to stand up in front of a conference and read more of his writing without having to go through such a detailed process. Although he still needs help, Reg now considers himself able to read.

The authors have seen many examples of adults first encountering symbols, by writing about themselves. This piece by Mabel is one such piece. She wrote it with help, partly using on-screen grids and partly dictating, but her response to the finished article, hearing it read to her by the computer and then holding the printout was overwhelming. She was just so excited.

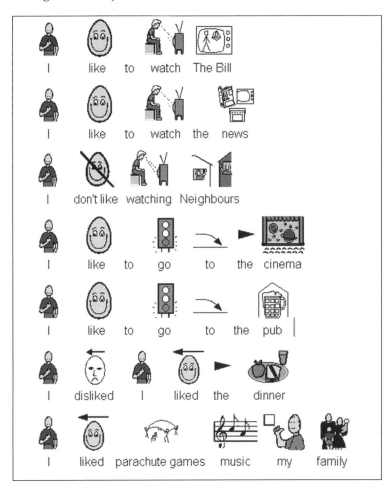

Figure 3.6 *A piece of writing by an adult using on-screen grids and some help*

5. Selecting a symbol vocabulary

Chapter 2 described some of the symbol sets that are currently available. Which symbols are appropriate in any context will depend on the user, the environment and the context for use. In the past two or three years, there has been quite a change in the general attitude to vocabulary. Many professionals are taking a more 'user-centred' approach, drawing on the range of images available according to circumstances, and accessing the range of vocabulary needed. The fact that so many symbols are available electronically is very useful.

In many places, adults with more severe learning difficulties are supported by a total approach to communication. The Somerset Total Communication uses speech, sign or gesture and symbols together to reinforce meaning to try to help the participants understand as much as possible. For this reason they have supplemented the standard sets of symbols with specific images relating to the local environment and activities. Symbols are introduced as they are needed by an individual. The learning is always in context and so is much more likely to be understood. A similar approach has been taken by Jacqui Corker and Judith Rice from the Honormead Schools, Rotherham, to provide a coherent communication service (Corker and Rice 1996). The Makaton Development Project has used signs and symbols to support spoken language for many years, including the use of illustrations of signs to help non-signers to communicate in this multi-modal context. Longwill School in Birmingham support signing with graphical representations of signs. Other initiatives, such as Signalong are also adding symbols to complement signed vocabularies.

Clearly, care still needs to be taken in choosing vocabularies. Where symbols form a major part of the user's means of communication, the choice of vocabulary is of vital importance. It will need to include social as well as curriculum language. Allen *et al.* (1992), examining the selection of vocabularies, maintain that the choice of symbols should be determined by the interests as well as the needs of the user. They stress that 'Communication is "fun". The first sign/symbols introduced should be those which are highly motivating for the user.' And that, 'The ritual selection of mundane signs/symbols for "food", "drink" and "toilet" are hardly likely to fire the child's imagination if these needs are routinely met' (1992: 33).

The overall appearance of the work is another factor to consider. Where the symbols are presented in games on cards, there is little problem. However, a page of writing using a very mixed set could look a mess and be very distracting. There is more discussion of this in Chapter 7, in the section on accessible information.

The symbols that you choose, and they way that they are presented to users will depend upon the circumstances. Yasmin Shah, from Bradstow School in Kent has very clear principles upon which the symbol work in that school is managed:

- We use coloured PCS symbols as a rule as we find that our students understand them a lot more readily than Rebus or Makaton symbols. We also draw from other coloured symbol vocabularies. Sometimes we do use Rebus symbols, depending on how transparent they are.
- We only use the symbols for key words. We will bold and increase the font of frequent words (to develop word recognition).
- We do not use symbols that are very iconic unless the student is able to understand them relatively easily.
- We double space the lines. This results in text and non-text being visually separated so that they are easy to read.
- We do not, as a rule, use symbols of tense indicators. For example, we will use the symbol for 'walk' then F1 1 to 'walked'. The time arrow is not meaningful for many of our students.
- We will try to use symbols that are clear for our students. Thus we will use 'go' for many words. This means that whoever is preparing the non-text material needs to have a sensitivity for language, and should be familiar with the symbol vocabulary so that they can choose appropriate alternatives. I have found that working closely with staff as well as formal training have enabled development of good 'translation skills' of words to symbols.

- In evaluating choices of symbols used I will cover the text and ask other staff if they are able to 'read' the symbols. I find that this is a good way to determine clarity or 'transparency' of the symbols.

She concludes:

It is very exciting seeing some students who have been so resistant to reading really enjoy decoding symbols. I hope it will be the beginning for them of discovering both the pleasure as well as the knowledge that is available in a wide range of reading materials.

In other situations the pupils appear able to handle quite extensive symbol coverage. Clare Martin believes that it is the right of students to have a symbol available for every word that is presented. She finds that the youngsters read the symbols they understand, and the more abstract symbols, which tend not to carry so much information, can be ignored, but those students who are trying to read a complete article in the newspaper, for example, want to have a representation for every word that is spoken. Gill Lloyd concurs. Initially, she used to support just the key words, but her more able students like to feel that they are able to access all of the text rather than a 'telegraphic' version. The key in all of these cases is to use good plain text, in short sentences, so that whatever the support, the message is clear.

Although some of the early familiarisation activities presented line drawings or symbols without the accompanying text, it is certainly desirable to add the word to the symbol as soon as possible in the familiarisation process. By always including the word with the symbol, from the earliest stages, the reader may gradually build up a sight vocabulary. An added advantage is that the non-symbol reader is also immediately able to understand the meaning.

Generally in this book we have illustrated symbols with the word placed below the symbol. Some people prefer it the other way so that if a pupil is pointing to the symbol the word is not obscured. Writing with Symbols supports both formats.

Summary

In this chapter the emphasis has been on starting to use symbols through interaction. This interaction can take many forms: games, telling stories which are then written, as a part of conversation and through seeing symbols in the environment. The next chapter discusses ways in which symbols can be used in indirect communication, through reading and writing, as a step towards developing literacy.

4 Beginnings of literacy

The next step after acquiring a sight vocabulary of words or pictures is to begin to put them together to communicate. Information Technology has made symbols easier to handle for both teachers and carers and learners. This chapter looks specifically at how symbols are used to introduce reading and writing skills. The examples show how symbols can support text for students learning to read, and how they can provide a means of writing for users who are not able to use traditional orthography.

1. Enabling techniques

Reading materials can easily be made using computers, simply by typing into a symbol software program that has access to a set of symbols. Before the introduction of computer software to manipulate symbols, written materials were made either by hand-drawing symbols or by copying, cutting and pasting symbols individually. A few people will be able to draw symbols and, like writing by hand, will give it a personal quality. The advantage of this is that it is not dependent upon any technology. The disadvantage is that the symbols may not be drawn consistently, the memorised vocabularies may be small, and it is not easy to create extensive material.

Whilst some users may be able to create a small number of symbols by drawing, but realistically they will need to manipulate symbols that are already printed, either using cards or by using technology. The use of computer software gives access to very large vocabularies which can be selected either by typing the equivalent words or by selecting symbols from a set of grids on the computer screen or on a peripheral device attached to the computer.

Because so many of the examples of symbols being used for reading and writing have involved computer technology, it is necessary to explain briefly the techniques, devices and terminology.

Symbol software

Writing with Symbols 2000 (Widgit Software) is a computer program which works a little bit like a word processor, but, as you type, a symbol will automatically appear above (or below, depending on choice) each word for which there is a symbol. If there is no symbol, then the word appears on its own. There are a number of symbol systems that can be used with Writing with Symbols. At the time of going to press these were Rebus, Makaton, and PCS. These sets contain substantial numbers of symbols, for example, the combination of the Rebus Symbol Collection and PCS symbols gives a vocabulary of some 9000 concepts. There are also alternative symbols for many concepts, giving the option of a more precise representation. Alternatively, the Makaton symbols and graphic images of the signs can be similarly managed. Using such software it is possible to mix and match between the symbol sets and add your own pictures or illustrations. The appropriate use of digitised pictures, captured on a digital camera or scanned from a print, can considerably enhance the writing. This was discussed in Chapter 2. The key point is that software can give the writer freedom to work with their preferred symbols or other images.

There are two other aspects of computer software that improve its ease of use, and suitability for purpose. First is the ability to choose a symbol that most clearly represents the intended meaning, whether it is by giving alternatives, as described in Chapter 2, or by allowing single concepts which are described by more than one word – such as 'hair brush', or 'frying pan'. Second is the option to only add symbols to those words that need a graphic, so that the reader is not overloaded. Ideally, the software will give the writer a choice as they work.

Computer displays and feedback

Another advantage of using a computer to create symbol materials is the flexibility it offers in terms of display and feedback. Readers with visual impairment may find it easier to read large, thicker symbols, perhaps in yellow on a blue background, rather than the traditional black on white. A learner starting to use symbols may respond to large symbols, and the text may be presented in a small font, to support the word, but leaving the focus on the graphic. A reader at a later stage may focus on the text, but be supported by small images for key or difficult words.

The addition of speech to support the symbol and text writing can, of course, increase its accessibility for many users who are working on the computer. A learner may be motivated and reassured by hearing their words, either as they are written or as the whole document is read to them.

As the power of computer software increases, the kinds of features and feedback will also improve.

2. Techniques for writing

Computer technology is fine for those who can type and who want to produce symbol-supported documents for people with learning disabilities to respond to, either at the computer or printed out. However, symbol users need to be able to write as well. There are various lo-tech ways in which beginner writers can start to assemble symbols and words, and these will be described later in this chapter. This section looks at ways that the computer can help learners to write, initially with support, and eventually independently.

Amanuensis

The way that Reg started to write, using an amanuensis to actually key the writing in for him, is one of the main ways that early writers can start to see how texts are created, before they have the spelling and manipulative skills to do it for themselves. However, some professionals deny that this is writing. Our view is that the authorship is the essential factor, rather than the technique. An amanuensis may help the writer but one has to be very careful not to interfere. Jenny, a classroom assistant, works regularly with the students helping them to write in this way. She will test their concentration on the output by making 'accidental' mistakes. Their engagement is clear when they see incorrect or inappropriate symbols, and want them changed. She is also careful to work on the finished text with them, reading it back and checking that it is exactly what they intended.

This approach is especially helpful when discussing the students' choices. They may not always find exactly the right word, and her knowledge of the vocabulary can help them in this.

Overlay keyboards

An overlay keyboard is a touch tablet that connects to the computer. There are various ones on the market, but the most common ones are Informax, the Concept Keyboard, and Intellikeys. The principle behind these boards is that when an area of the board is touched, it will send a 'message' to the computer as though it had been typed from the keyboard. Before one of these boards can be used, a special file has to be created that contains the 'messages' that are assigned to each area of the board, and also a paper overlay has to be printed to show the user which key to press for each message. These boards come with the utility software to create these. It is not part of the symbol software although that can be used to create the paper overlays.

The advantage of these boards for beginner writers is that these displays can be quite large, and are flat on the table rather than on a screen, and are activated simply by touch. The disadvantage is that there is only one overlay available at a time, and so for many practical purposes the vocabulary is restricted to what can be presented on the single sheet.

Two boards are illustrated. One with a simple set of choices from Sally Adds, at Woodlands School, to write about working in the garden. When you press the area with the symbol of the leaves, the message 'sweep the leaves' is sent to the program. The other overlay is a much more complex one, that used for a group of adults to write about their experiences at a particular event.

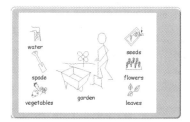 

Figure 4.1 *Overlay keyboards*

On-screen grids

The first step to independent writing may be through the use of symbols in on-screen grids. Such a grid would have a bank of symbols or symbol phrases that the user can select to add to the document.

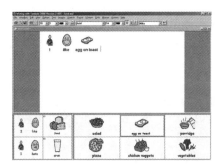

Figure 4.2 *An on-screen set of grids*

The two screens above show different stages in creating a document. The screen on the left shows a display with a simple grid for a beginner writer. There are two grids on the screen. The left of these gives a sentence starter 'I like' and two cells that are 'selection' cells. When the writer chooses the 'food', a grid with a set of food to write about is available, or if the 'drink' cell is chosen, the display will change, offering a set of drinks instead. Clearly more complex arrangements with larger numbers of grids can be made.

The next display below shows how grids can support a writer to express their feelings. In this case the writer is invited to select one of a set of three sentences that most clearly expresses their opinion. When one is chosen, a new set is displayed, for them to choose. This particular set will gradually build up a document that describes the type of work that a student might like to do.

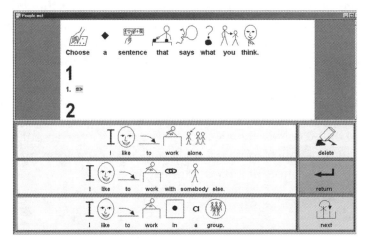

Figure 4.3 *Guided writing, with suggestions the student could choose if they wished*

Grids like these can be used with a mouse – where the writer clicks the mouse pointer on a cell, with a touch window, or they can be scanned so that a writer using switches as an alternative input can make their selection.

Voice recognition

At the time of writing, voice recognition technology is still somewhat in its infancy. The systems work well with users who have clear speech or very consistent reproduction. This is not always the case for users with learning difficulties. Another factor in the suitability of voice recognition will be the ease of editing. The voice commands required to correct mistakes can be more complex than might be appropriate for a writer at this level. However, these are the limitations of voice recognition systems, not of the software that can manipulate symbols.

3. The beginning of reading

Symbols can be used to introduce children to what the process of reading actually involves. The process is confusing to many children and sometimes needs to be taught explicitly. The fundamental principle of reading is that one can extract meaning from text. If children are introduced to the reading process by the use of symbols from which they find meaning readily accessible, then the principle is more easily understood (James 1993: 10–11).

Symbol stories and reading books

The activities described in Chapter 3 to introduce symbols will go a long way towards helping readers understand that the symbols carry meaning, but a particularly motivating route is through stories. Alison Carter, at Longwill School, Birmingham, for children with hearing impairments, used symbols representing manual signs to help her pupils read and re-tell familiar stories. They all knew the theme of Jack and the Beanstalk, and seeing the familiar ideas represented graphically helped them to understand the link between the representation and its meaning. Stories in symbols can be created to suit readers of different abilities so that readers in the same group may access the same story at different levels (see Figure 4.4).

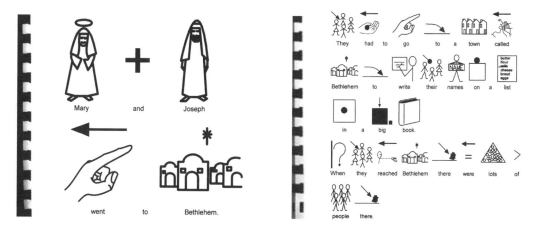

Figure 4.4 *Differentiated versions of the Christmas story*

A series of reading material for children, entitled *Inclusive Readers* (published by David Fulton in 2002), has big books illustrated with pictures and plain text, and these are supported with symbol versions of them at different levels that can be photocopied from the teachers' manual.

Figure 4.5 *Two stories from* Inclusive Readers

Very often the most successful stories are those that tell of familiar events and people, and may be very simply made from photographs with captions. Charlotte, one of a class of pupils at the Lambert School, Stratford-upon-Avon, has made her own reading book (see Figure 4.6). Photographs were taken of her doing lots of different things. She dictated the symbol phrase to accompany each one, and together they were put into a book. The teacher added a flap which covered the photograph, so that Charlotte could read the symbols and then uncover the picture to see herself. Children love pop-up books and books with windows that open. As well as providing additional motivation, of course it helped the teacher to check Charlotte's symbol reading.

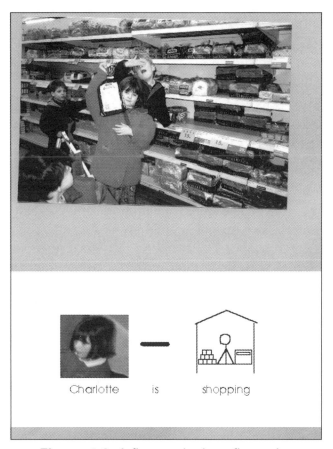

Figure 4.6 *A first reader by a first writer*

Existing stories can be adapted by adding symbol phrases or individual symbols into published storybooks. Several schools have done this for the early stages of the Oxford Reading Tree scheme (published by Oxford University Press). This approach also works for older pupils.

Figure 4.7 *A story from the Oxford Reading Tree, with symbol captions added*

We use stories with young children as a major way of introducing and rehearsing experiences and concepts. They are a crucial way of presenting ideas in a friendly, supportive and often quite simple manner, and in a way that real-life experiences may not always achieve. Children enjoy hearing familiar stories, in which they can anticipate the events and participate in its telling. Children with literacy difficulties, who are not acquiring sight vocabulary and who may find detailed pictorial illustrations a bit complex, may be helped by the addition of symbol support for the text.

Pati King-DeBaun, writing about storytelling between parent and child, suggests that the important bond created by successful verbal interactions may not develop effectively where the child is non-verbal or communicatively delayed. 'Some studies suggest that the less able, non-speaking children receive fewer and less stimulating early literacy experiences' (King-DeBaun 1990: 1). She presents a wealth of ideas through which children with communication difficulties can gain more positive reading experiences through adaptations such as symbolised stories, big books, as well as the use of video and slide stories. Big books are ones in which the pages from a story have been significantly enlarged so that a group of children, possibly in wheelchairs, can share the book together. She suggests that although further research is needed, 'It is believed that providing the non-verbal and communicatively delayed child with the means to interact effectively with the story time situation can begin to create the once lacking positive bond to early reading experiences' (ibid.: 1).

The grid in Figure 4.8 shows the key vocabulary for a popular story *Bears in the Night* (Berenstein and Berenstein 1972). This story provides reinforcement of prepositions. The bears go out on an adventure and in doing so go 'over', 'under', 'up' and 'down' things. This grid can be used for joining in with the story, where the child can point to missing words. Used with a computer it could be used to rewrite the story and to show comprehension. Like many popular stories this has a small and repetitive vocabulary, making it ideal for a first reading activity. A communication aid could be used with the overlay above to take part in telling the story.

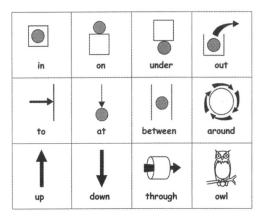

Figure 4.8 Bears in the Night *with a communication grid*

This kind of support can help students at different levels of literacy, increasing the possibilities for differentiation. The symbols can provide clues to some of the text, helping the struggling reader. In addition, they provide more complete information for the non-reader, who can use them to understand the content of each large picture.

In the nursery and early years classes at Wilson Stuart School they make a lot of books. Like Charlotte's, these are mainly communication books with photographs and symbol descriptions. These books are used sitting and talking with a carer or teacher and are made by putting each page into a plastic pocket to make it durable. These are put into ring binders which allow pages to be added in the right sequence. The staff have found that it is important to choose the plastic pockets carefully so that they do not have reflective surfaces. Many sorts are too shiny which makes reading difficult.

Students creating their own books is one way of overcoming the problem of having age-appropriate materials for older pupils and for adults. Several years ago, in the very early days of symbol use, Steve Cullingford-Agnew, working with a senior class of pupils with severe learning difficulties, created some excellent non-fiction materials for the school library. A particularly good example was their road safety manual. The students took pictures of safe and not-safe places to cross the road, in and around their own locality. They then put these pictures into a book that could be used in teaching road safety to younger pupils. The advantages of this are obvious – a sense of value and self-esteem for the authors, producing real books, and a valuable resource of relevant materials for the school.

Shirley Austin, the special needs co-ordinator from Marshlands School, Hailsham, used pupils' own symbol books to encourage reading and writing. They dictated short stories which were pasted into small books, one sentence to a page. These were photocopied so that the pupil could read their story and draw pictures to illustrate

Figure 4.9 *Poem by Shirley Austin*

it, copy the writing, or add other words. Having multiple copies meant that each pupil could use their own book and have the pleasure of using somebody else's – extending the reading to new vocabulary. They also made attractive books to take home. Shirley has extended much of this work to give support to a range of pupils. She uses poems with repetitive sounds to encourage reading.

As each pupil becomes familiar with a poem, he or she will go on to do a range of literacy activities based on that vocabulary. These may be worksheets with sentences to finish or cloze procedures. Completing an activity independently gives a feeling of being able to achieve something without help, which eventually raises self-esteem. The child may even read the poem to the class when very familiar with it.

One of Karen Slade's pupils wrote a wonderfully creative story with the help of symbols about a lion who had lost his mane, which he illustrated with drawings. The boy was a reluctant learner, and she tried this approach to motivate him to write and tell stories. They wrote together. He enjoyed seeing the symbols, and it helped him to re-read the writing. This approach gave him the means of showing his full capabilities in a long and interesting story.

Figure 4.10 *Symbols can encourage a reluctant writer*

Dialogue and collaborative work

Many people enjoy acting or joining in group activities. Plays written in symbols can stimulate many drama activities. The script below was used by the students acting in a Christmas play. Each player had their part printed in a different colour. This enabled them to see their own part and helped them to follow as others read their lines. The text might be written in full, but it could simply act as a reminder for lines almost learned, or even for some improvisation!

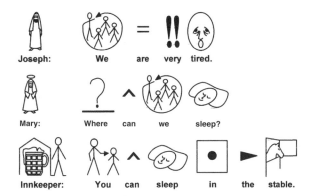

Figure 4.11 *Dialogue can help pupils work together and collaborate*

One group of students used symbols to tell jokes. The symbols reminded them of the punch lines. They also used to make up silly stories, in the manner of a game of consequences. One person would read a story with lots of missing words. Each time a word was needed it was supplied by taking a card from a pile. The activity provided more than just a laugh. It encouraged a sense of what was right and what might be incongruous, it encouraged interaction and co-operation, and provided a game which was not teacher controlled. There is further discussion on ways in which symbols have been used to stimulate a conversation and decisions in Chapter 6.

4. The beginning of writing

Much of the discussion on beginning to read has explored reading through readers building their own texts. There are specific tasks to developing writing skills, however, which are outlined in the literacy strategy, that look at the technicalities of building texts:

Word level work – word recognition, matching and word building

There are many activities that can help children learning words; some can be done with simple lo-tech methods using cards and games, and there are computer programs that will help with a host of spelling, word-building and word recognition activities. Here are just two:

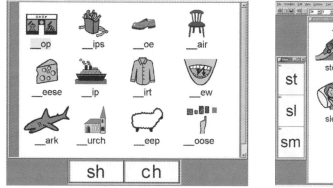
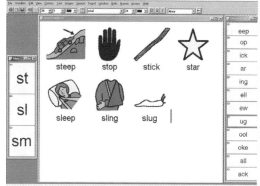

Figure 4.12 *Two word-building activities on computer*

Older students learning to spell may need tasks which provide greater motivation, and where the content may have greater relevance or interest. A student returning from work experience first wrote his account using an overlay keyboard with symbols so that he wrote largely by symbol selection. He had some ability to write with traditional orthography and his teacher created an activity based on his initial writing. She removed words from the writing, leaving the symbol clues (see Figure 4.13). The student then completed the passage again, this time by filling in the gaps by typing letters from the keyboard.

Figure 4.13 *A student's own writing used to reinforce literacy learning*

Sentence level work – building sentences and starting to use grammar

Captions like the ones in Charlotte's book can easily be made from overlay keyboards or on-screen grids. The vocabulary is limited, and the repetitive sentence sequencing reinforces sentence building. Starting with cards and lo-tech methods is often the best initial approach for users who can manipulate them. Cards with different coloured background representing subjects, verbs and objects, give a clear visual structure to the sentence. The example in Figure 4.14 takes this idea further. It is about describing a scene.

Figure 4.14 *Building a sentence from individual symbol cards*

When we write a sentence describing something, such as the picture in Figure 4.14, we are really doing a number of things. First, we choose the words, then, we sequence them, finally, we translate each word into a series of letters. The problem of choosing the ideas and then sequencing them can be made quite separate from the next task of representing each word by letters. The use of symbols as a means of rendering problems into smaller steps which can be dealt with singly, is a theme which recurs in this book.

Using a mixture of sentence building and familiarisation games the reader will gradually come to understand that some symbols represent objects or people, others represent 'doing' words, and eventually that some symbols are descriptive. Here are three ways that teachers have helped children build sentences.

1. Symbols were coloured according to the John Horniman colour coding scheme. Verbs were coloured yellow, pronouns were green, etc. The pupils first chose a person, then a doing word. Later they were able to extend the phrases with more words. Sometimes they made sentences to match pictures in stories they knew and other times would play games together, one child writing a sentence and the other reading it out.

2. Overlay keyboards were used with the vocabulary relating to some large colourful pictures. The pupils used the overlays to describe things in the picture. Some pupils used Writing with Symbols so that their descriptions were illustrated, others used the symbols on the overlay to help them choose the correct words which were written into an ordinary word processor. This

53

intervening step appeared to give the pupils confidence in choosing less familiar words, which they were then able to read back from the printed text with little help.

3. A set of on-screen grids was constructed so that the first column had people, the second actions and the third had objects. Within each cell were incidental words, such as 'The', 'My', etc. so that the pupil could focus on the structure of the sentence construction.

Text level work – constructing a whole document

We have looked at some of the techniques that may help the physical task of writing. Some children will need help in constructing texts. The symbol stories in the Inclusive Readers books (see Figure 4.5) have a single sentence per page. One of the support resources contains each of these sentences ready to be printed onto cards, plus the illustrations for the book. One text level task is to sequence the lines of the story and the illustrations, to re-construct the text. This activity helps the reader understand the meaning of the story in greater depth, having to consider and make decisions about each separate statement.

This chapter has already discussed ways in which banks of symbol phrases and sentences on computer could also be sequenced to build a longer document (see Figures 4.1, 4.2 and 4.3). These banks give the writer some choices, rather than having to start with a blank sheet of paper or screen. They may provide material for the whole document or act as a story starter.

Instead of having to start from scratch, a student may be more confident re-writing a familiar text, where there is a core of familiar vocabulary, and possibly illustrations, already provided. These techniques allow students to develop skills in composition and writing for an audience without being dependent upon spelling and individual letter skills.

Other strategies include collaborative writing, where students can work together to generate ideas and enthusiasm. The concentration and energy level of students working together may work to exceed what they might achieve on their own. Carol Allen believes in the power of collaboration and has worked with groups of students to construct longer stories and even a novel in symbol-supported text. She wryly remarks that the first chapter, in which she had the greatest involvement, is by far the dullest!

5. Using symbols with 'readers'

Some children learning to read may use symbols simply as cues for spelling activities and support other reading and writing tasks. The advantage of symbols is that they offer a wide vocabulary, and in this context do not need to be seen as part of a 'system' since it is quite possible to restrict their use to those that are easily recognised. In a letter describing her work, Frances James, co-author of *On First Reading* (James and Kerr 1993) writes, 'Learners who are having difficulty acquiring traditional orthographic skills do not have problems of linking symbols to meanings – that is why symbols are such a gift, it takes a burden off the children/adults.'

Another burden that symbols can remove from beginner readers is the organisational skills they need. For some children, the complexities of understanding and following the task compound the difficulties of the task itself. Barbara Hunter, an outreach teacher from Wilson Stuart School, uses symbols as part of a strategy to help the Year 1 children she supports in mainstream schools so that they can focus on the real learning task in hand. Instructions are written with symbol support so that they are not penalised if they cannot accurately read the instructions. The example in Figure 4.15 shows the care with which she plans this, telling the child which hand to use to start the task, so that a weakness in physical co-ordination is not a limiting factor in the numeracy task in hand. She will expect the child to read some of the task, but the symbols are there for reinforcement, they don't have to be used, but by having them, one child does not have to be seen to be 'different' because of the resources they need.

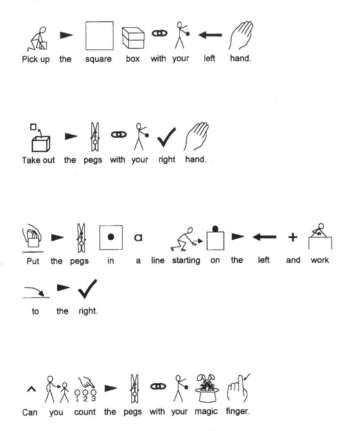

Figure 4.15 *Symbols may help with the practicalities of an activity*

Sue Norton of Deerswood School, West Sussex, did a study into the effectiveness of symbols when used to support pupils with poor literacy skills in a secondary MDL school. She found that although there was a wide variation in the degree to which a pupil's accuracy or comprehension was enhanced, it did seem likely that there was some real benefit to pupils with poor literacy skills. The symbols provided additional cues about the text, and she believes that they helped the pupils to interact with the texts more effectively, for example, by being able to locate information more readily. In the MLD context she found no difficulty of attitude to symbols, but would be cautious about this aspect in a mainstream setting.

6. Sharing information

As well as access to both formal and private writing, an important part of familiarisation with reading and writing is having access to a wide range of materials such as newspapers, newsletters and community publications.

Access to community information through newspapers is extremely valuable, provided, of course, that the material is accessible to the intended readers. Many schools are now producing symbol newspapers. Perhaps the most well known of these papers are the ones produced by students at George Hastwell School, who, as far as we know, were the first symbol newspaper writers. The paper is produced each school term, by the senior class. The editorial team decide who is going to gather news, who will be responsible for different tasks, and generally plan and manage the whole production with as little help as possible from their teachers. The result is a lively account of the activities of students and staff as well as other topical items that interest the editors.

George Hastwell School have been publishing their newspaper since 1991. The first one to use symbols was published in 1992, when the technology became available. One copy of each edition is reduced to A4 size, laminated to make it durable, and placed in the library. In this way they are beginning to build up an archive for meeting the requirements of the history curriculum as well as providing interesting relevant reading material.

Figure 4.16 *The cover item from the tenth anniversary edition of the George Hastwell newspaper*

Not all students my be able to read all of the contents, but using photographs, drawings, symbols and words, there will be enough material to engage each student in some of it. News-4-You is a weekly newspaper from the USA that can be downloaded from the web. This has topical items, jokes, stories and activities. It is now available in two levels. The easier level comes with a communication grid to help interaction between the reader and carer. There is more on information-sharing in Chapter 7.

Probably one of the most effective ways that readers will acquire literacy skills is simply through exposure, having symbols, pictures and words in as many places as possible. Items like these newspapers can help considerably and add to the status of symbols.

Summary

Although this chapter was principally about beginning to read and write, whether with graphics or text, it necessarily examined some of the strategies and techniques that help people with learning or motor difficulties access these tasks. It has also looked at some of the many ways in which reading and writing can be encouraged in a variety of contexts. The next chapter looks at ways in which symbols may enhance access to the curriculum for pupils in schools and in Chapter 6, there are examples of symbols providing support for older students in further education and adults living in the community.

5 Access to learning

A great deal of information has been denied to people with learning disabilities because of their difficulties in understanding or using standard text. This chapter looks at the role of symbols in supporting access to learning, particularly in relation to school curricula which in the UK includes the National Curriculum. In Chapter 6 the attention focuses on older students with a learning disability in their transition from school to the adult world, and in developing the life skills necessary to participate in society.

1. The role of symbols in learning

Most school-based learning takes place through the spoken and written word. We live in a very verbal society. Pupils who experience difficulties with these media will have difficulties throughout the whole of their education. McNamara and Moreton (1990) note that there is a tendency to deliver the curriculum, particularly in history, geography and science, through reading and writing. They found that 'it is the very emphasis on reading skills that holds children up in their academic progress' (ibid.: 7).

> One of the major aims of education must be to give children maximum autonomy in their environment. Reading is one of the ways in which this can be achieved. By broadening the definition of reading to include the extraction of meaning from symbols, as well as from text, such autonomy can be offered to a wider range of children. (James 1993: 10)

The development of literacy is, therefore, of prime importance. However, if we are to help pupils with poor literacy skills to engage in the whole curriculum and to acquire other knowledge and understanding, we need to take steps to minimise the problems that literacy difficulties cause. This will impact both on the learning and the motivation of pupils with difficulties. There appears to be a close correlation between pupils' reading ability and their self-esteem (Chapman *et al.*, cited in Macnamarra and Moreton 1990).

Symbols can provide a useful tool in breaking the cycle of underachievement.

> Symbols enhance the participation of students with learning difficulties in a range of social and educational activities. They help to bring a sense of achievement, a precious tool in building self-esteem, and as such can make a valuable contribution to the lives and education of those with learning difficulties. (Carpenter 1995)

Carpenter and Morris (2001) and Abbott (2000) write extensively on ways in which symbols support communication and access to literacy for pupils with severe learning difficulties. Some pupils may use symbols as part of an alternative and augmentative system. For other pupils, symbols can give the means by which they can begin to develop literacy skills and access the full range of learning while some of the more intractable difficulties are being addressed. The very steps which provide access to learning across the curriculum will also provide the opportunities for developing literacy and a way which allows pupils to perceive their own development.

2. Supporting differentiation

> Many pupils with learning difficulties are placed within a mainstream school, or within a teaching group with a very wide range of learning difficulties … [This will] present teachers with the challenge of differentiating the teaching material so that it is accessible to all the pupils in the group, and of ensuring that all the pupils are able to demonstrate achievement and progression. (Martin and Gummett 2001: 83)

One infant class uses a range of materials to include all pupils at circle time at the beginning of each day. As well as collecting individual news, there is a general discussion about the weather, seasons and environment before moving on to discussion of the practical details of the day's activities. Pupils are encouraged to share their observations, such as birds in their garden, buds appearing, leaves falling, animals they have seen, as well as personal, local and national events they are aware of. The contributions are recorded by the teacher writing on the board and by pupils selecting symbols or pictures to illustrate their ideas. Presenting the material in pictorial, oral and written forms helps to accommodate the varying levels of reading and speaking ability within the group. The display stays up for the rest of the day, so that it can be looked at from time to time. This is a great help to some pupils who need a concrete form of communication to overcome the ephemeral nature of speech.

3. Supporting the curriculum

We have already discussed many strategies in which symbols can help children to construct and explore meaning in a general approach to developing literacy, through having reading materials and tools for writing. In the next sections we will illustrate how these strategies have been applied in specific curriculum areas.

English

The use of symbols to develop specific orthographic skills at word and sentence levels was discussed in Chapter 4, as well as the creation of symbol stories both by and for pupils with reading difficulties. This section will look particularly at ways that symbols may enhance access to literature.

In 1997 we wrote about first uses of symbols to bring poetry to pupils with severe learning difficulties. Since then it has become a normal part of exploring literature. That first example, which was from George Hastwell School, was written in the spring of 1992. Their school is in Cumbria, where William Wordsworth lived. Clare Martin translated this well-known poem for the group to be able to share in reciting it together. (Golden was represented by a piece of gold foil from a sweet wrapper.) It was at the time when the daffodils were in abundance and the pupils very much entered into the spirit and enjoyed the activity.

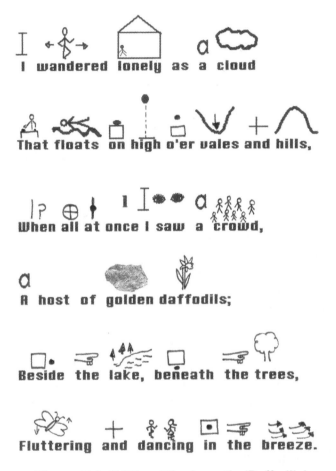

Figure 5.1 *William Wordsworth, 'Daffodils'*

Since then, the school has brought a wealth of poetry to their pupils through their Literacy Summer Schools, described by Abbott (2000).

Other poetry has similarly been symbolised by teachers. The symbols may simply act as a reminder of the language, but for pupils who have difficulty reading and remembering, they can help to bring richer language within their grasp. Clearly some poetry lends itself to symbol support better than others. This poem by W.H. Auden ('Funeral Blues') has clear concepts which make it easy to find symbol representations which can convey the same meanings.

Figure 5.2 W.H. Auden, 'Funeral Blues'

However, another well-known poem, 'The Tyger' by Blake, is more difficult. Although each individual word can just about be represented, the meaning of phrases such as 'fearful symmetry' may well be rather difficult for the reader. Simply rendering the poem in symbols will not necessarily make the concepts more accessible.

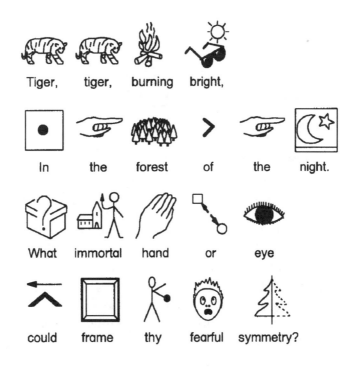

Figure 5.3 William Blake, 'Tiger, tiger'

61

Strong rhythms and rhymes can help language development, but often the only 'poetry' given to people with learning difficulties are nursery rhymes. Older students will need material which is more age appropriate. The examples above show that with the picture cues to help, it is not difficult to make this important form of literacy accessible across the age range. West Oaks School, Sheffield, project the words and symbols for the hymns they sing onto a screen. They did this at the Harvest festival to help families as well as the pupils from the school, in the same way that the symbols support the words of this popular Christmas song. In both of these contexts only the key words were given symbols. In this way the readers were given enough prompts to remind them of the words without the display being visually cluttered.

SNOW IS FALLING
by Shakin' Stevens

Snow   is   falling   all   around   us

children   laughing, having fun.

'Tis the   season   for   love   and   understanding

Merry   Christmas   everyone

Figure 5.4 *Shakin' Stevens, 'Snow is falling'*

Grove (1998), in *Literature for All*, shows how imaginative approaches to the introduction of classical literature can enhance quality of education. It may not give the full and true text, but young people with learning difficulties are being introduced to classic texts. Students at George Hastwell School have performed versions of *The Tempest* and *A Midsummer Night's Dream*. *The Tempest* was performed by students using puppets. It is clear that the students were deeply involved in the productions and gained a great deal from the experience. They wrote their own symbol version of *The Tempest*, adding photographs of their puppets for the characters. The characters in the symbol version of *A Midsummer Night's Dream* were represented by photographs of the pupils in costume.

Collaborative writing

As well as individual creativity, collaborative writing can contribute to literacy and vocabulary development. Pupils without speech who use communication aids can find it difficult to join in collaborative work and discussion. At Wilson Stuart school they have a special Communication Group, that has sessions together in which they develop these skills.

Poetry, and story making are some of the ways that these nine-year-olds are encouraged to communicate. The group meets weekly with the aim of encouraging peer-to-peer communication. It has successfully worked on collaborative writing projects, including poetry. The pieces below are from a series of pieces in which they wrote about things they liked.

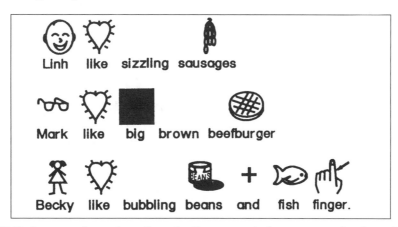

Figure 5.5 *A poem based on Rap rhythms, made by communication aid users*

Figure 5.6 *An example of collaborative writing stories from a communication group*

Although these examples illustrate support for the English curriculum, obviously this strategy is appropriate in many areas of learning. Other collaborative writing projects have been explored elsewhere in this book.

Comprehension

At a more technical level, understanding of texts, and writing reviews or commentaries can also be supported by symbols and by technology. This comprehension sheet made for *The Very Hungry Caterpillar* (Carle 1970) asked questions in a way that allowed the answer to be selected from two alternatives.

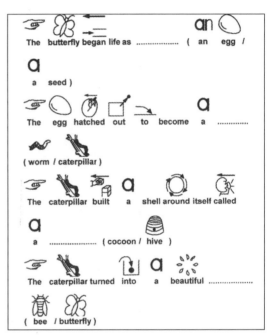

Figure 5.7 *Comprehension activity on* The Hungry Caterpillar

Gill Lloyd, from Ashwood School, used stories about familiar events and experiences to encourage reading, and supports this with worksheets. This example is the worksheet from a story about a day in the life of a postman. There is an activity for the students to do after reading the story in which actions mentioned in the story are matched to clocks showing the times that events took place.

The communication boards described in Chapter 3, which helped pupils to join in story telling, can also be used to show comprehension. Putting the same vocabulary onto a computer overlay keyboard or on-screen grid lets the pupils both retell the story in their own words or answer questions about the meaning.

As well as straightforward comprehension, book reviews can demonstrate comprehension, maybe by creating a pro-forma or template to complete, maybe through an on-screen questionnaire. Symbol illustrations provide prompts for the symbol reader and for the student who is using symbols as a support for their reading as described in Sue Norton's work (see p. 55). Building a collection of reports can give a sense of accomplishment and an opportunity to review work done over a period.

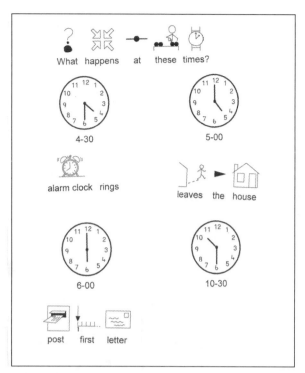

Figure 5.8 *Comprehension activity on a story with 'stick-on' cards*

History

A study of the Vikings by a group of secondary-aged pupils used a wide range of resources including an e-mail link with a school in Norway which produced some first-hand information.

The study was extended by the availability of a set of symbols to support the Viking study. Pupils were able to use the computer, some with the help of an overlay keyboard, to produce their own written material to include in their booklets on the Vikings. The pupils enjoyed being able to read from their booklets in a group, and in order to include a pupil who had no speech, some phrases about the Vikings were programmed into a communication device. 'His response indicated that he was pleased to be able to join in with the other pupils' (Martin and Gummett 2001: 87).

Figure 5.9 *Symbol writing about Vikings*

Figure 5.9 shows writing which used a symbol for each word. Others may choose to symbolise only the key words.

A project reported by the Curriculum Council for Wales (1991) explored ways in which the history curriculum could be made more accessible to pupils with learning difficulties. Although carried out some time ago, this project was one of the first in which teachers started to use symbols to enhance curriculum access, and still gives a good illustration of how pupils can access new concepts. In this project the pupils were provided with symbols of several artefacts used in the Victorian era. They were asked to identify the items and suggest what they were used for. This activity prompted an animated discussion between the pupils. They were then asked to identify the comparable item used today. Various games were devised such as snap – between modern and Victorian pairs, or grouping items by category from the same era.

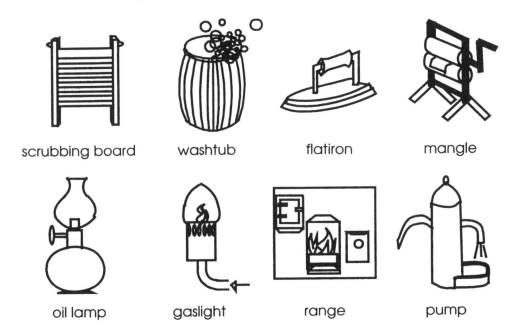

| scrubbing board | washtub | flatiron | mangle |

| oil lamp | gaslight | range | pump |

Figure 5.10 *Symbols of Victorian artefacts. Clip-art, drawings and scanned images could supplement the vocabulary in this context*

A large cross-section of a Victorian house and of a modern one were also drawn and the items were placed in the appropriate rooms in the house of the associated period. This exercise showed that the pupils had grasped many of the differences between today and the Victorian era, for example 'the iron went in the living room because it was heated on the range' (Curriculum Council for Wales 1991: 27).

Mary Parker and Christine Wright from Ysgol Ew'r Delyn, Cardiff, who devised the activities described above, wrote:

> When [symbol software was] introduced for use with communication impaired pupils it became clear that this software could be used to enable such pupils to participate in other National Curriculum areas. This was the first opportunity many pupils had to record their work independently and the printed work provided a record of their achievements. (Parker and Wright 1991: 1)

Another activity from the project used symbols to illustrate events and artefacts concerned with the Battle of Hastings. The pupils were asked to identify each symbol, to use the symbols as prompts to re-tell the story of the battle, and then to sequence the events of the story. They used an overlay keyboard which told the story in four simple steps. The teacher told the story using the overlay as a visual aid, and then the pupils retold the story at the computer, pressing the areas on the overlay to show the correct sequence of events. Pupils also added symbols and their own pictures to photocopies of the overlays, to add information to the story.

66

Parker and Wright explained that the use of this type of differentiated material gave the pupils 'access to programmes of study followed by their peers in mainstream schools. Differentiation within the National Curriculum has enabled the pupils to accomplish tasks consistent with their level of attainment and has ensured that all pupils achieve success' (ibid.: 8). This still holds true today.

Geography

Weather is a popular aspect of geography. Leo Berry from the Lambert School made a set of weather symbols which could be temporarily stuck onto a plastic-covered map of the country. The pupils in the class would role-play the television weather reporters, giving detailed accounts of the local and national weather forecasts. Symbols used in this type of activity were obtained from a variety of sources: copies of those used on the television, printed sources such as weather reports in the newspapers, and those used in the general symbols sets available in school. There are no reports of this eclectic approach causing difficulties in classrooms. Teachers tend to choose the most appropriate symbol for each purpose and present that to the group.

The same issue arises with map symbols. These looked at different sorts of maps to understand what they meant, including examining the map symbols, then they wrote about their experiences using yet another symbol system.

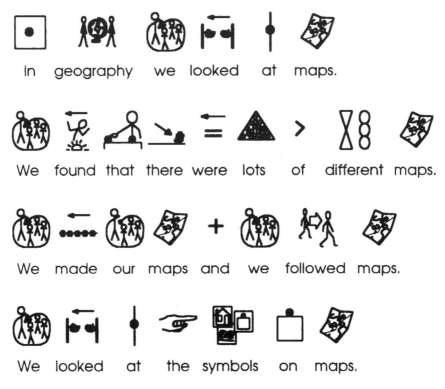

Figure 5.11 *Group summary of curriculum activity*

Worksheets produced with symbols give these pupils the chance to complete their own work, using symbols for just as much support as they need. They can also support off-site activities and field trips.

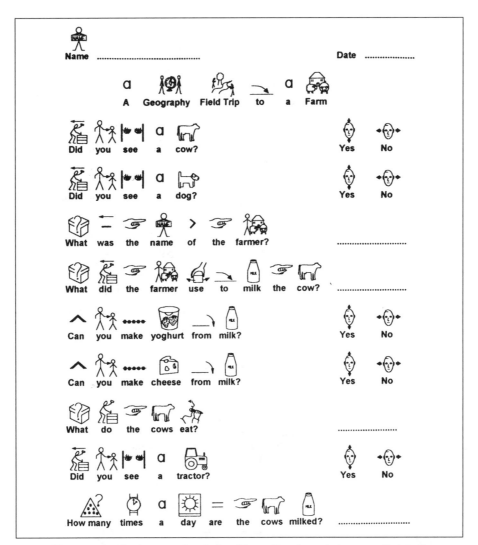

Figure 5.12 *A questionnaire for collecting data on a field trip*

> Some pupils with learning difficulties may not be able to recall all the symbols but, nevertheless, will be able to understand sufficient symbols to gain an overall impression of what is written … The addition of symbols will allow the pupil to recall the work that they did during that theme, even some years later. In this way, pupils can become actively involved in their own Records of Achievement. (Gummett and Martin 2001: 95)

The cross-curricular theme of 'Dwellings' explored by a class of secondary-aged students with severe learning difficulties involved the use of symbols in many activities. The students carried out a survey of where people lived, using a data collection sheet with symbols prompts. Another group used an overlay keyboard to construct house specifications in an activity based on an estate agency. They were able to think not only about what features their houses had, but also about their geographical locations. The overlay helped them to decide by offering options from which they could select. Selina's report contained a variety of materials: information provided as part of the class resources, data sheets which she filled in, and writing which she created on the computer or with help from her teacher. She included information on where people in her class lived, where famous people lived, where her favourite television programmes were set, and information on different kinds of homes. Finally, she designed her ideal future home. All her work was bound into a book which contained a rich variety of material on the subject and showed that she had used a range of techniques for gathering and recording information.

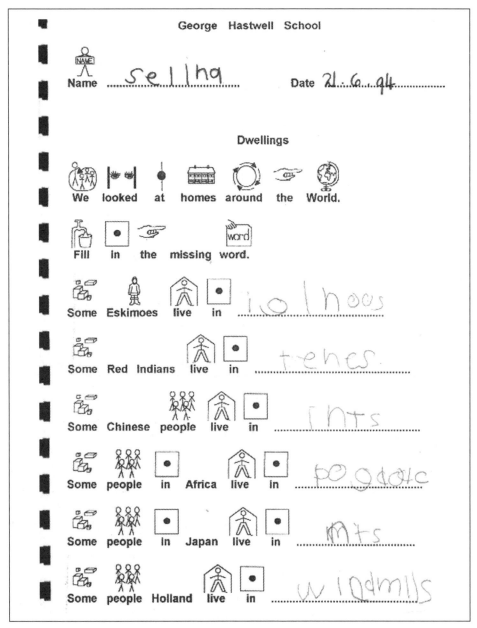

Figure 5.13 *A completed data collection questionnaire*

Modern foreign languages

Many schools now have foreign language events such as a French Day, or a Euro Week. These events are aimed at bringing the language alive by using it in many contexts, both educational and social. On a French Day at a school in Berkshire, pupils decorated the school hall to look like their idea of a French café. Staff and pupils were encouraged to come and try different foods, ordering *en français* of course. The use of symbols with the French text underneath helped many of the pupils to achieve this without help. The French Week at George Hastwell School was such a success that French has become a regular feature on the school timetable. Communication aids which can reproduce recorded speech were programmed with a range of French phrases which the pupils could activate by touching the appropriate symbol overlay. This particularly helped pupils with communication difficulties – less confident pupils and many parents who visited the café were relieved to be able to use them.

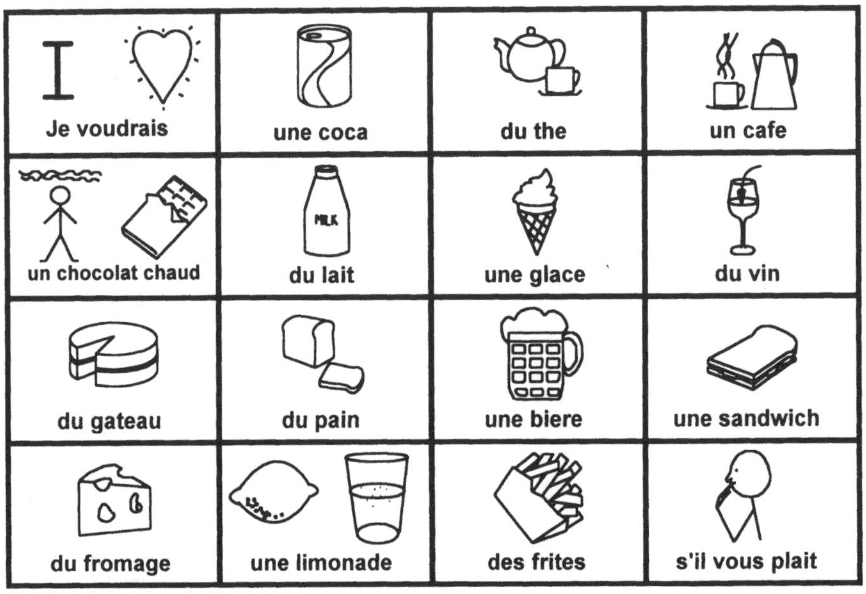

I ♡ Je voudrais	une coca	du the	un cafe
un chocolat chaud	du lait	une glace	du vin
du gateau	du pain	une biere	une sandwich
du fromage	une limonade	des frites	s'il vous plait

Figure 5.14 *Overlay used to order in the French café*

Pupils also produced their own written work with French text using the same symbols. This showed that the pupils understood the context and were able to create appropriate writing in response to set activities. Without the symbols it is unlikely that many of the pupils would have been able to engage purposefully in these activities. The French speech helped them to hear the differences in pronunciation. It also caused great amusement when they listened to the English text spoken with the French accent!

At Heronsbridge School, Bridgend, the inclusion of symbols has given improved access to the written word for their less able pupils. The teachers wrote: 'Obviously the fact that they are already familiar with the symbols from their general work bridges the gaps and helps our pupils with greater difficulties understand the concept of a foreign language.' Using the computer, pupils copy-typed phrases, which were reinforced by the spoken word. They also built up their own sentences, demonstrating an ability for free writing 'which has always been the most difficult aspect of teaching a foreign language to pupils with severe learning difficulties'.

Clearly, all the early literacy strategies discussed for using the student's native language can apply in learning a foreign language. In Canada symbols are being used to support pupils in immersion schools, where the pupils are learning to be bilingual. Ben's is an unusual situation in that he teaches in the French School Board in Nova Scotia. French Canadians make up 4 per cent of the Nova Scotia population but they are fiercely proud of their heritage. They are working really hard to preserve their culture and language. Through the schools, they are hoping to strengthen a weakening community and children that are being brought up by English television and in English communities. The children come to school in kindergarten often knowing no French. They are immediately immersed in French but the challenges of meeting regular curriculum standards in what, for the children, is a foreign language, can be staggering. They are really embracing the French version of Writing with Symbols to help them bridge the gap.

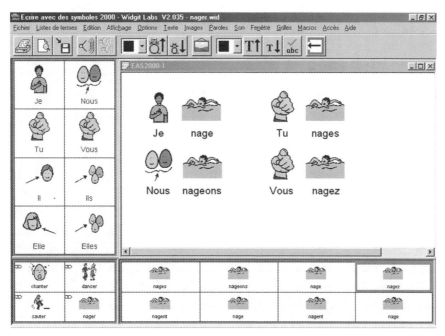

Figure 5.15 *Practising French conjugations*

Religious, moral and social education

At Key Stage 2:

> Children should be developing a greater understanding of themselves and an awareness of the needs and feelings of other people from a variety of faiths and cultures. Symbols can not only help to communicate at the basic word level, the images themselves can communicate information about the other cultures. These visual images may help the children to appreciate the different symbols used in other cultures. (Brown 1996: 154)

To show similar concepts across the differing faiths we can use extensions of the kinds of conventions used in designing symbols, which were described in Chapter 2. For example, the basic symbol for 'pray' was based on 'please' and 'thank you' with the symbol for the particular faith. Places of worship are represented by either a pictorial representation, as in church or mosque, or by the generic symbol for building with the faith symbol enclosed. Symbols in Figure 5.16 help the pupils to identify items from different faiths.

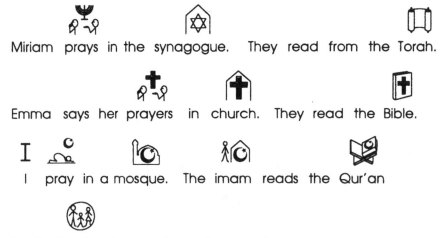

Miriam prays in the synagogue. They read from the Torah.

Emma says her prayers in church. They read the Bible.

I pray in a mosque. The imam reads the Qur'an

Paul's family does not go to church.

Figure 5.16 *Writing on different faiths in a Year 5 mainstream class*

It is important to be able to share experiences from outside school, and the development of symbols representing different cultures and customs will help this.

Many of us find expressing emotions difficult, especially if those emotions are associated with pain or grief. Talking about very personal feelings is often very hard, and these problems will be compounded by additional communication difficulties. People experiencing loss or change in their lives need to find mechanisms for sharing their feelings. Symbols, images and artefacts can often help to provide cues and prompts, but sometimes people can be helped by being given phrases or ideas from which they can choose the most appropriate to their need, rather than having to conjure the ideas up for themselves. Stories which tell of similar situations can also help to give people the mechanism by which they can start to explain their own fears and hopes.

Jamie 's teacher said they will do a project about monsters. They will work in groups.

Jamie did not want to do this. He was afraid.

Figure 5.17 *The story of Jamie, used to explore feelings*

The story of Jamie is adapted from one of a series by Janine Amos (Amos 1995). It is part of a series of books on feelings. At the end of each story there are questions to help discussion. The full story is read to the pupils, but the symbol version allows the pupil who finds reading difficult to be reminded of the story. Sometimes it is necessary to re-read a story several times to consider its meaning. The symbols help the pupil to do this independently. A teacher using this story wrote:

> One of the younger children asked to read [Jamie's Story] and clearly used the symbols as cues. He called it a weird book but said it could have been about him – except that he would not think a dinosaur is a monster because, he says, although he finds reading hard, he is clever and would not make that mistake.

A young lady with learning difficulties read another story which described the day that Grandma died. By reading the story with her father, she was able to consider the subject and ask questions in a supportive environment. Often, difficult subjects like this are hard to raise, and can get left out or avoided until too late. Brown (1999) describes ways in which children can be engaged in some of the rituals surrounding important events to help them understand what is going on. Getting them to express feelings through drawings and also having stories such as the one about Grandma, can help them relate to the events and their emotions.

Children who find it difficult to manage their emotions can be very disturbing and disturbed. Shirley Austin uses symbols with her readers to help them explore their feelings in relation to social events. The school ran a course for pupils with behaviour difficulties encouraging them to think and talk about their feelings in different situations. A series of worksheets helps them think about their own, and other people's behaviour (Figures 5.18 and 5.19).

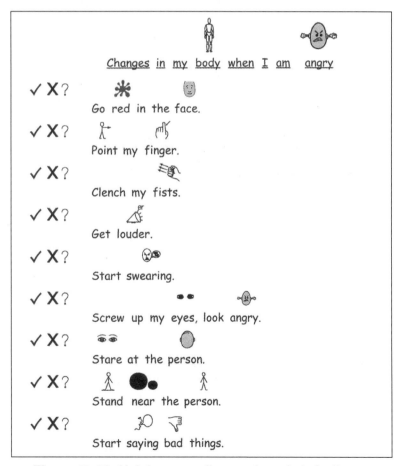

Figure 5.18 *Helping a pupil to explore their feelings*

This activity asks the student to record what happens to them in certain circumstances. She says that although many of the pupils can read, the symbols help then to be sure exactly which question is which, and saves them having to admit when a word is not clear. The focus is on the task, not on their literacy. The 'attitude' cards shown in Figure 1.4 are also part of the set of resources for the course. At the beginning and end of the course the students filled in a questionnaire.

Figure 5.19 *An extract from the student questionnaire*

They compared the number of angry/happy/sad faces and both the staff and students were surprised to see that the number of angry faces had gone down significantly for some children. Although it had not been planned this way, this sheet turned out to be a very good assessment tool.

Science

As part of a science project pupils looked at how people grow and change as they get older. They looked at photographs of people at different ages from newborn babies to old people. Figure 5.20 shows the instruction sheet to explain how the photographs should be sequenced, helping them to also relate the symbol to their understanding of age.

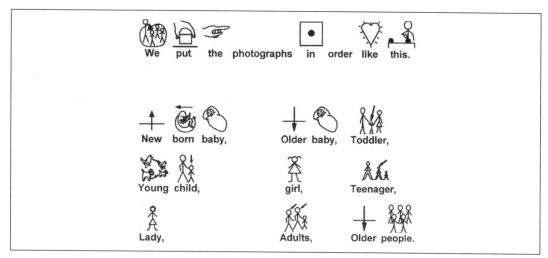

Figure 5.20 *Describing the process of a study or investigation can help understanding of the entire project*

Gathering data over time has important lessons for understanding. Weather reports recorded yesterday and today can be used to predict the weather for tomorrow. By building up a record of weather over several days, the pupils can get some idea of the changing patterns. They can be encouraged to look backward and forward over time, to understand the idea of a prediction compared with what actually happened.

Sue Norton is the science co-ordinator in a secondary school, and finds that her students can be helped significantly with symbols, not because they need them for most of their reading, but because the symbols remind them of the concepts. The alternative symbols for circuit will help pupils at different levels. When they see the symbol for 'volt' the picture of the man pushing visually reminds them of what voltage is.

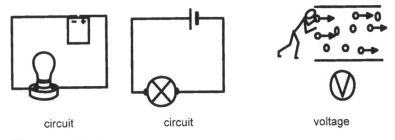

Figure 5.21 *Science symbols as a reminder of the concepts*

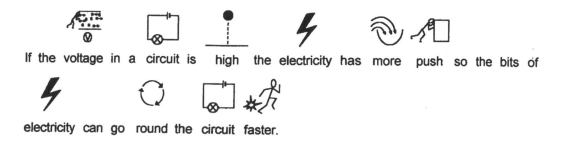

Figure 5.22 *Science of revision materials*

Sue has created an extensive set of revision materials that use symbols, and has successfully taken her students through GCSE using these techniques.

Some science concepts can be represented by symbols or very simple line drawings. Others are more complex and may need more detailed pictures. Other ideas are just too complex, but at least if we can help the students to remember some of the concepts with these visual aids, then their learning will be enhanced. This raises some interesting questions about symbol development: who should be involved, what is sensible, where the limits may lie, but most significantly, it illustrates that the symbols can act as a reminder but cannot by themselves teach the concept.

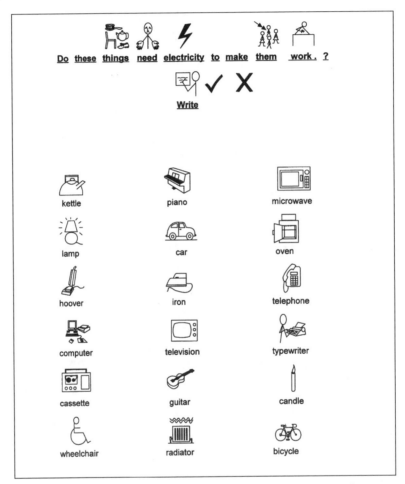

Figure 5.23 *An activity sheet suitable for students working at a less complex level*

Food technology

Food technology is an area in which many pupils with learning difficulties, given support, find it easy to achieve. There are many examples where symbol recipe cards, reminders on hygiene procedures and cooking preparation have enabled increased levels of independence. Some of these are described in Chapter 6.

Katie, attending food technology classes in a mainstream school, had great difficulty following what she was supposed to do. She understood quite a bit about cooking, and could work well if she could also see what the others were doing. Katie's learning support assistant observed that once Katie was organised, she could follow what was going on by watching the others. She made worksheets that Katie could use for practical activities. The one shown in Figure 5.24 first tells Katie what equipment she needs and then, because she finds decisions difficult, the choices are listed separately. They found this strategy gave Katie a head start in this type of activity, enhancing her inclusion.

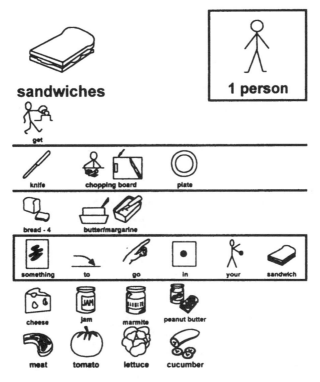

Figure 5.24 *An instruction sheet to help a student organise the equipment needed for an activity*

Katie was also helped by having the cupboards labelled so she could find things quickly and put them away! The symbols helped other pupils in this task too. This strategy was successfully extended into other curriculum areas, such as science, so that she could join in most practical activities.

Data handling

Pupils need to learn to record and manipulate data across the curriculum. The examples below illustrate how symbols can provide that bit of additional support for the less able pupil, without changing the level of the basic activity, for example Figure 5.25 gathers data on pets, but could deal with virtually any topic. The traffic survey (Figure 5.26) might have boxes above the symbol for each type of vehicle in which to record each sighting, so that the totals can be counted later back in the classroom. A histogram can be easily made by colouring the boxes.

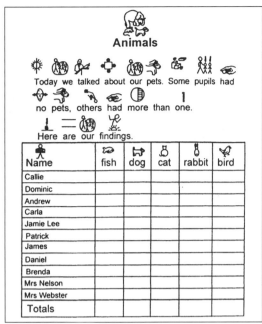

Figure 5.25 *Collecting data about pets*

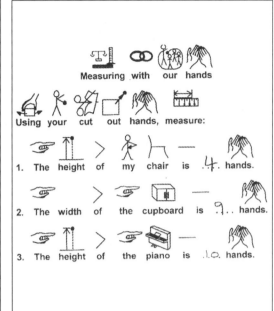

Figure 5.26 *Collecting measurement data*

A measurement activity required the pupils to draw around and make cut-outs of their hands and to use these to measure things in the classroom. Jamie used this worksheet to record his measurements.

The data, once collected, can be displayed in a variety of formats. In Leo's class the data were entered into the computer. Carla counted four leaves, and typed in the word 'leaf' four times. This gave her satisfaction in typing it correctly, but also helped in getting a feeling for the 'fourness'. They also used symbol worksheets for reading and sorting activities, for example, a page of symbols and words with different garments was made for choosing appropriate clothes to wear on a cold winter's day.

At a simpler level, the activity may require the student to sort data into categories. On-screen grids can make this a very straightforward task, allowing the pupil to focus on the sorting rather than the recording skills.

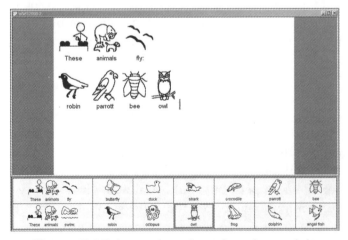

Figure 5.27 *A computer-based sorting activity*

4. Assessment and recording achievement

It is important that each pupil's record of achievement should cover all areas of their individual curriculum ... and that these records should continue to be meaningful to the pupil, even years after they have been compiled. The use of photographs and video can help to achieve this, as can the use of information technology in conjunction with symbol writing software (e.g. Writing with Symbols 2000 from Widgit Software). Indeed as Sebba (1994) points out, 'Records of Achievement capture part of the pupil's own personal history'. (Martin and Gummett 2001: 82)

Gill Lloyd at Woodlands School, Ashtead, was one of the pioneers in the use of symbols for recording achievement some years ago, working with the awarding authorities to gain acceptance of alternative forms of communication in the official record. This now seems commonplace, but serves to remind us how opportunities have changed in recent years.

Two examples of Records of Achievement (Figure 5.28) show how pupils at different levels of literacy can still express their capabilities.

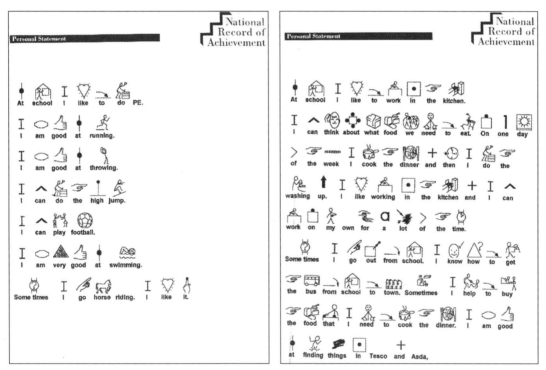

Figure 5.28 *Two Records of Achievement*

Summary

Many of the examples in this chapter have shown symbols being used with pupils who have quite severe difficulties in developing literacy. It has shown that opportunities can be created through the use of symbol support. It has also shown that teachers are finding that on occasion they have had to question their previous assumptions on individual capability, and to raise their expectations of individual potential.

6 Developing independence

Probably one of the areas of most significant growth in symbol use in the past few years has been for young people and adults with learning disabilities in preparing for and living in the adult world. A few years ago, many adults with a learning disability were not encouraged to make choices and develop their own opinions. Since then we have seen an amazing increase in opportunity brought about by improvements in post-16 education and in the number of local schemes for adults.

1. Being in control

One of the most important steps towards independence is developing a sense of self. Having a sense of what is happening, and what is going to happen, can make a big difference to an individual's feeling of control. Most of us feel uncomfortable when we are unsure of what to expect or what is going to happen, and we feel put out when the expected does not occur.

At Woodlands School students are involved in planning the activities for the following week.

> Each Friday morning the students and staff from the F.E. group plan the following week's activities together. The group splits for some activities and is based at college and leisure centres for others; some opportunity for negotiation is built into the session. Students are informed ahead of time of planned changes in the timetable and can help with the planning and organisation of the group.

> As each day is discussed key information points are typed into the computer using 'Writing with Symbols' software and at the end of the session everyone is given a copy of the sheet and a further copy is placed on the door for reference.

> The aim is that everyone has a means of checking on what is happening each day which they can share with parents and supply staff, and which will help them to remember what to bring with them.

> Support work for this is done in cognitive sessions when students use the concept keyboard or question sheets and answer questions based on the activity sheet and

their knowledge of the weekly routine. This helps them to become familiar with extracting information from a familiar written (here symbolised) source.

Parents have been known to phone and ask for a copy of the activity sheet if they have not received one. Students sit on the bus reading the sheet together and talking about what they will do. Individuals have looked at the sheet to confirm that they are going shopping on Thursday. Students always know who is to cook lunch/go shopping/make drinks when asked. The symbolised sheet presents information in visual format which supports and reinforces the discussion; the students do look at the sheets with parents and alone and remember what is written. The sheets are valued and the students do make sure they get a copy. (Lloyd 1996)

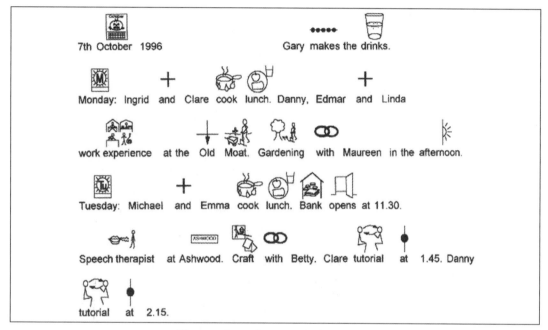

Figure 6.1 *A record of activities*

Being in control may be a matter of having the right resources or vocabulary available. Rebecca Marriott is a young lady without speech, who attends college. She is supported by her mother, Wendy, and Speech and Language therapist, Judy Mellon. Their first aim was to help Rebecca communicate more. They have done this through lo-tech methods, creating communication books. The first books Rebecca used each covered a particular topic – college (or school as it was then), holidays, family, etc. The format comprised a photograph on one side of a small album, and a page of eight symbols on the other. Anybody communicating with Rebecca could use the book to ask questions, which Rebecca could respond to by pointing. These books enabled newcomers to immediately engage in conversation with Rebecca – a process which would not have happened otherwise.

Housework
Friday
Register
Hello
butter
flour
milk
cheese
bread
eggs
List
Housework
Wash
Hoover
Ironing
Drink
Writing
Dinner
Register
Walk
Talk
Writing
Music
Assembly
Bus
Home

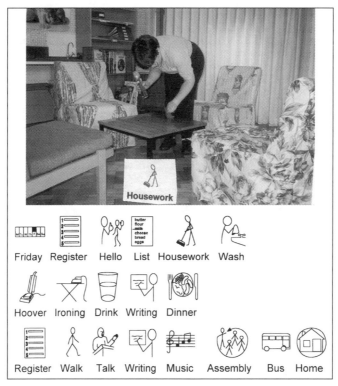

Figure 6.2 *A page from Rebecca's communication book*

As time has gone on they have refined the books and are working on a single one with laminated pages. Rebecca is learning to navigate around this book, which can, of course, cover a much more flexible vocabulary range than a series of individual books. The choices are becoming more complex, and she is able to build sentences from individual symbols on a sheet such as this one:

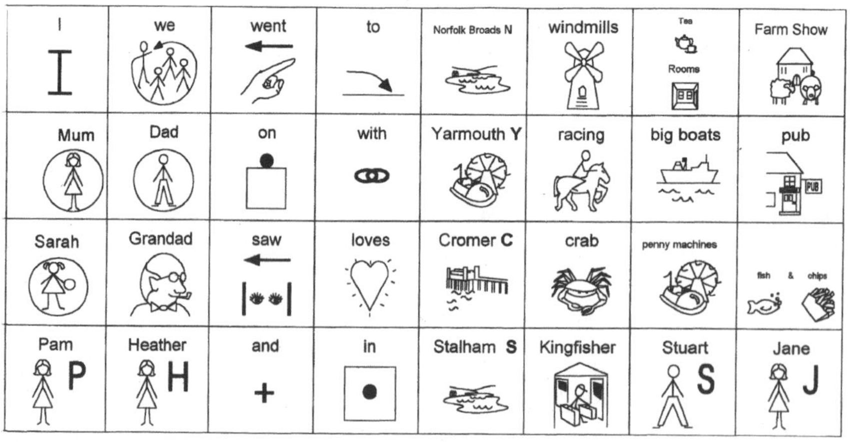

I
we
went
to
Norfolk Broads N
windmills
Tea Rooms
Farm Show
Mum
Dad
on
with
Yarmouth Y
racing
big boats
pub
Sarah
Grandad
saw
loves
Cromer C
crab
penny machines
fish & chips
Pam P
Heather H
and
+
in
Stalham S
Kingfisher
Stuart S
Jane J

Figure 6.3 *A page of more vocabulary for more general conversation from Rebecca's book*

This sense of control is very evident. She is always asking to add new pages, write about new experiences, and is actively involved in choosing the vocabulary she wants. She constructs letters and records working with her mother and using the communication book. She has recently started using the computer to construct her own writing. She can sequence phrases to write about what she does each day. Although her literacy skills are developing, the most significant aspect of this work is the communication opportunities this gives Rebecca, and the ability to be part of a group.

2. Self-sufficiency

Another step towards independence is to increase the level of personal involvement in each activity or process of the day. We want to encourage students to do as much as possible for themselves, and to be a little less dependent upon others. There are difficulties in this. Each individual has a different level of capability, and will develop or mature at a different rate. Some young people will have a sense of excitement at facing new challenges, others will be afraid. Older people, who may have had more supervised care in the past, may feel insecure facing changes. Schools and colleges, dealing with groups of adults with very different needs, have to plan carefully how these steps to independence can be made within the educational setting. There are the limitations of staffing and resources and there are also supervision responsibilities. For parents and carers there are other concerns. Sometimes they may fear the consequences of increased independence. With more opportunities may come additional risks, and these have to be balanced carefully against the more structured approach which can be achieved if carers and parents take more decisions themselves.

Timetables and personal planners can be extremely helpful in developing self-sufficiency. These devices are much more than lists of activities. They can help the students to prepare themselves, both physically and mentally. Mental preparation removes feelings of dependency, while reminders, such as what to put in the swimming bag, or take on a camping expedition, can help students develop organisational skills and to take responsibility for their own equipment (Paveley 1993).

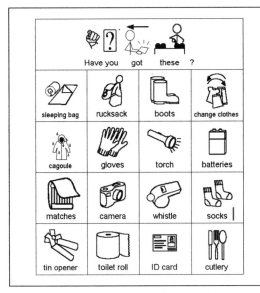

Figure 6.4 *A reminder sheet*

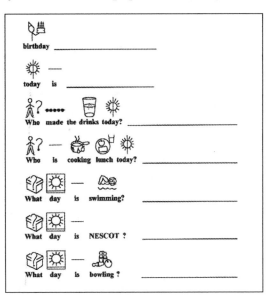

Figure 6.5 *A checklist to see what a student remembers*

After a number of years in institutional care John now lives in sheltered accommodation in the community. He has not been used to looking after himself at all and frequently would forget something important. Typically he might fail to switch off his cooker. His day centre would make notices to remind him. They would be pinned up in strategic places, and he was given a checklist to go through before he went to bed or before he went out. These notices made a significant difference to John's independence. Without them he would forget essential actions, and staff at one time were concerned about his safety in such an independent setting.

Organising oneself through notices and reminders may seem very obvious, but they can be very valuable. However, just as we discussed the power of Alan's writing in Chapter 1, the more the user can be involved in creating the timetables, lists or reminders, the more likely they are to understand and remember them. Writing has a very important role in the development of these skills, not just as a means of recording, but also as a tool for developing memory and for structuring thinking. Take a trivial example. We may write a shopping list, only to find when we get to the supermarket that the shopping list is still on the kitchen table. We remember most of the list simply because we have written it. The process of writing has helped us with the cognitive task of remembering. At another level we may make notes of a meeting, conversation or lecture. The act of making the notes, re-articulating the ideas for oneself, helps to structure these ideas in the mind, as well as serving as a reminder at a later time. Talking also helps us to structure our thoughts. We explore ideas through conversation, and where the concepts are difficult, we may use somebody as a sounding board to help us to articulate these ideas.

A person with a disability, which hinders or prevents these processes, will be further disadvantaged by being denied access to these support mechanisms. Note taking, recording events and conversations, and sequencing new ideas will be harder without the power to write. Similarly, a communication difficulty is likely to make conversation difficult, again reducing the opportunity to rehearse ideas and thoughts verbally.

It need not be like this. In the last section it was demonstrated that people with a learning disability *can* write. Lists can be made with cards by marking specific symbols in a list or, using a computer, it is possible to create one's own list from a selection provided. A group homes organisation were awarded Lottery funding to put a computer with symbol software in each of their residential homes. One of the key activities in relation to the homes was the rota of domestic tasks that the residents did. Until the introduction of the computers there, rotas were made by the care staff. Using the computer with symbols the rotas could be printed in a much more understandable format. The photographs of the residents and the symbols representing the tasks were printed out onto an overlay keyboard so that the residents could write the lists themselves. There was a very positive and unexpected outcome from this because the residents started to take much more control over their participation. The warden remarked that most of the interaction was really between resident care staff rather than peer-to-peer. When they were making up these rotas the residents started to argue. They also used printouts of previous lists to settle arguments – an amazing step forward.

A common strategy is selecting cards from a bank and putting them into small holders, such as credit card wallets. These can be used discreetly but are still very functional.

Students using symbols in further education departments use writing as a major strategy for developing their thinking skills and understanding. When they have done the shopping for their meal, the students at Woodlands Schools have to record how much money they took with them, how much they spent and what was left.

At George Hastwell School they use the computer to practise money management. Here is part of one of their keyboard overlays and a worksheet looking at prices at McDonald's. This example was made some time ago, and prices have changed!

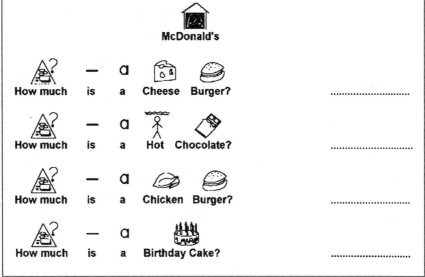

Figure 6.6 *Activities to help understand money*

The overlay gives the menu and price list which can be used with the computer to write choices, or it can be used as a menu and price list for completing the worksheet. The grid in Figure 6.7 was created for an adult. It was laminated and stuck onto a wheelchair tray to allow the user to place his own order in McDonald's, and, as Anne Hancox says, 'to also encourage some choice making'. She has made similar overlays for communication aids.

Figure 6.7 *A simple grid to encourage choices*

Anne, like many other people, has taken a similar approach to shopping lists and other situations where a basic communication vocabulary might be useful, encouraging people with a communication difficulty to express their own choices. Making decisions is not always easy, especially for people who have spent a long time in institutional care. It may be confusing to a user to know when there is a genuine choice available, and when the choices are 'restricted'. Quite simple techniques can be used to produce resources to support simple decision-making and choice.

3. Finding a voice

Being part of society implies involvement. Communication between individuals is an essential part of that involvement. Many people with a learning disability have communication difficulties which inhibit conversation. Opportunities are needed to stimulate conversation between all members of the group, not just between a learning disabled person and adults or carers. Students often need encouragement to communicate with each other and considerable care has to be taken by teachers to ensure that this happens.

Gill Lloyd makes much use of symbol cards including using them to develop self-sufficiency. Some of these are used to describe practical tasks, such as how to make coffee, other drinks, simple cleaning tasks, and so on. These have the advantage that they can be carried around while tasks are being done. Other cards are designed to help the young people develop conversation skills, and improve interaction.

She has devised sets of symbol question cards (see Figure 3.4). These may ask practical questions such as 'When do we go swimming?' or 'Do you have any pets?',

'What makes you cross at home?' or encourages opinions, like 'What makes you cross at school?' These are asked in a group situation. To start with, the students select a card, read it, and then answer. The next time they are encouraged to ask a partner, and finally the idea of asking a supplementary question is introduced ' Have you any pets?', 'Yes?', 'What do you have?', etc. The students are strongly encouraged to communicate with each other and the teachers avoid taking on the role of an intermediary. Gill says that often the students are so used to closed questions, they need practice to develop their conversational skills.

Linda Edwards, from St Piers in Surrey, works with the students to create communication passports. A communication passport is a document carried by a person with a communication difficulty and it describes how they like to be treated. It explains how to communicate with them and gives some background information such as their likes and dislikes. The aim is to make it easier for new people to communicate with them. A communication passport may use photographs, symbols, clip-art and whatever else conveys the necessary information. Communication passports have proved to be an important tool in easing communication, and increasing confidence of newcomers who may be insecure interacting with a person with a communication difficulty.

The Makaton Vocabulary Development Project (MVDP) has introduced an innovative scheme to train people who have a learning difficulty to become Peer Tutors. The Peer Tutors are taught how to communicate with others who also have learning difficulties. They work with friends, carers and professionals to enhance the communication of others with learning difficulties. Some Peer Tutors work in their own centres while others have been able to take on wider roles, working with professionals in different agencies. They are supported through this process by trained Makaton Tutors. The initiative has provided an opportunity for everyone in an establishment to be involved in enhancing communication skills. This approach will develop the self-confidence and communication skills of those who have been trained and shows that having a learning disability does not prevent someone from taking a full and responsible role in society.

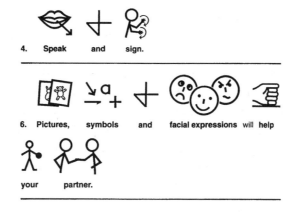

Figure 6.8 *An extract from the Makaton Peer Tutor guidance*

As well as having the mechanisms for communication, it is necessary to have something to say (Kiernan *et al.* 1987). It is very easy to focus very closely on the self-help areas, developing those skills which will enable the individual to accomplish more on his or her own. However, part of increasing independence must be to increase awareness of the world, and a growing sense of involvement may be assisted by widening the range of conversational topics in which the individual can participate. Bovair and Robbins (1996) identified a useful list of conversation topics. Although the list was drawn up to identify areas for conversation in teaching modern foreign languages to pupils with learning difficulties, it is valuable as it describes everyday topics suitable for developing understanding, communication and literacy for learners across all ages. It is likely to form the core of the programmes of study for many students with learning difficulties in post-16 education, and indicates vocabulary areas in which there should be a comprehensive range of symbols available.

a. Everyday activities
the language of the classroom
home life and school
food, health and fitness

b. Personal and social life
self, family and personal relationships
free time and social activities
holidays and special occasions

c. The world around us
home town and local area
the natural and man-made environment
people, places and customs

d. The world of work
language and communication in the workplace

e. The international world
life in other countries and communities

(Bovair and Robbins 1996: 111)

There are many different ways that people are encouraged to express opinions and choices. It may be a simple tick list of items, rather like a shopping list. It may be a questionnaire with spaces for pictures to be stuck in. Clifford, from Borehamwood Day Centre, is encouraged to express opinions by writing about his likes by making a list. The text list is written with help, and then a symbol is chosen so that when he reads the list back he is clued into which sentence is which. His list of favourite things shows the wide range of activities that he engages in (Figure 6.9).

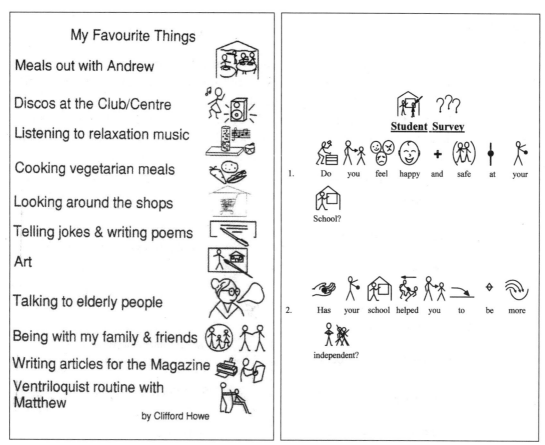

Figure 6.9 *Clifford's list of favourite things*

Figure 6.10 *A student survey with symbol support*

One can also use a full-scale survey with many different questions. The survey in Figure 6.10 has some 22 questions plus other response items. The survey was created as part of a research project looking into the 'value added' by the extended 24-hour curriculum. The guidance suggests that students answering the survey will want one-to-one support with a familiar and trusted adult who would explain and interpret the questions to the student. A symbol-supported version of the survey was prepared so that students could more easily follow some of the questions, and has space so that responses could be added in picture, symbol or other format. Ian Burtenshaw, from St Piers School, who made the symbol version, also made tick lists that the students could use to pick out responses, giving the students a variety of means of expressing their views. It was not intended that students would be able to read the questions accurately and unaided, but that the symbols gave a greater means of involvement, and thus independence, in answering.

Ian also designed a booklet that the students can fill in to help them prepare for their annual review. It starts by explaining what the review is, and why it happens. There are some general open questions, and then some pages that can simply be ticked. Students are particularly familiar with the symbols that represent activities, places and people in the school as these are used widely, and many can complete much of the document themselves.

4. Being heard

Sometimes there is a sudden need to have a voice and be heard. The communication book in Figure 6.11 was made very quickly to help Joyce in hospital after she had a stroke. The symbol cues were added so that staff and friends could be confident that Joyce had indicated the message she wanted. It didn't matter that Joyce had never seen symbols before. It was practical and functional. Fortunately it wasn't needed for very long, but it certainly made life much less frustrating at the time.

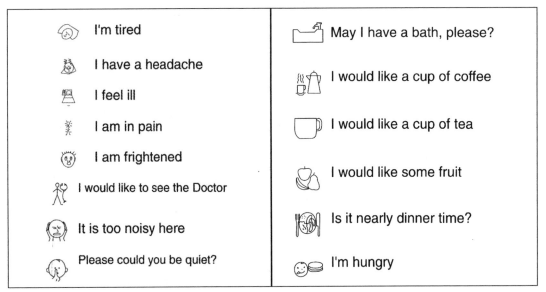

Figure 6.11 *Two pages from the communication book for a stroke patient*

Participation in society is not just a matter of communicating needs and wants. It is about achieving and having that achievement demonstrated. Mittler (2001) suggests that pupils with learning difficulties leaving school are likely to encounter many obstacles to their participation in society. 'Perhaps the biggest obstacle is the continuous pervasive underestimation of their abilities' (ibid: 329).

5. Assessment, accreditation and recording achievement

One way to have one's voice recognised is to be able to demonstrate capability. Accreditation and formal records of achievement are an important aspect of this. There are a number of accreditation schemes that are being made suitable for adults with a range of learning difficulties.

ASDAN (Award Scheme Development and Accreditation Network) provides a framework for developing and accrediting personal skills. The first step is a scheme called Transition Challenge, which focuses on helping young people move into the adult world. Towards Independence is their post-16 scheme which takes these skills further. It offers a selection of 22 modules to develop and accredit independent living skills. There is now a comprehensive set of modules with symbol support across these areas. Sally Murphy, who is involved with developing these materials, explains that many of the students on the scheme are familiar with the symbols from school, and being able to carry on using them at college provides continuity and reassures them that they will be able to understand the tasks as independently as possible. In addition to the more familiar independent living skills, some of the more recent topics added to the scheme include personal autonomy, self-advocacy, positive self-image and personal development.

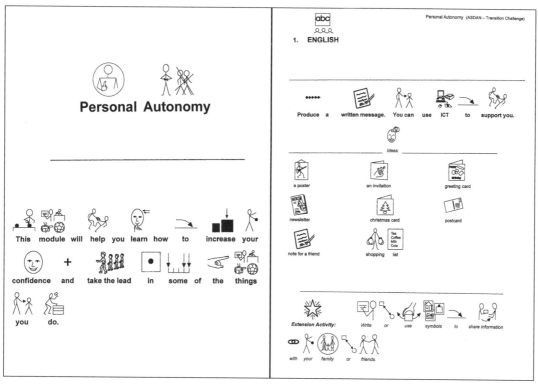

Figure 6.12 *Asdan's Transition Challenge: the first pages from the students' materials of the Personal Autonomy module*

Accreditation for Life and Living Skills (ALL) offers another scheme for accreditation of student capability. This scheme is a framework for curriculum development and for accreditation of curricula developed in individual institutions. It is designed particularly for students aged between 14 and 19 who have severe or profound learning difficulties. However, the framework is applicable to a more extended age group. As a framework it can be used in different ways, but many of the activities will be supported by the use of symbols.

Assessment of students is very much a process that involves communication and negotiation. In both formative and summative assessment symbols can help to structure and enable the communication processes necessary for assessment to be worthwhile. For example, at Woodlands School:

> students also work towards their preliminary access certificate. When they are confident they can complete a task independently, a formal assessment is arranged. Symbol worksheets help students to record their formative work and the assessment plan is written in this way and signed by the student and teacher. It is the record of the meeting and therefore needs to be accessible to candidate and assessor. (Lloyd 1996)

West Suffolk College have also used symbolised sheets to help in formative assessment. Andy Carmichael writes: 'I am sure we have not always got the balance right (number of symbols, correct synonym use of symbol, etc.) but it does work in practice!' The example in Figure 6.13 shows part of a sheet that students use to record their achievement in the computer course.

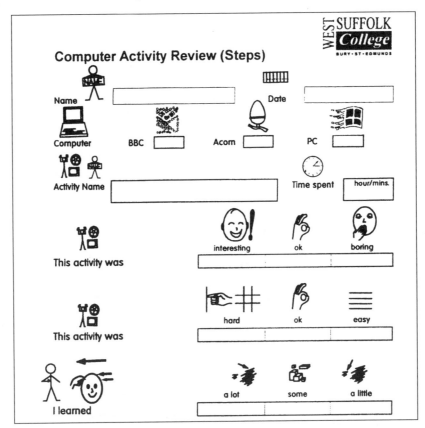

Figure 6.13 *A self-assessment form for IT capability*

All students at West Suffolk College have a code of conduct which they undertake to try to abide by. Symbols are used to give the students with learning disabilities access to this document. Andy has used one page of the A5 booklet for text and has used the other page for symbol statements. In the next chapter we will look at this means of using symbols where text and the corresponding symbols become 'unhinged'.

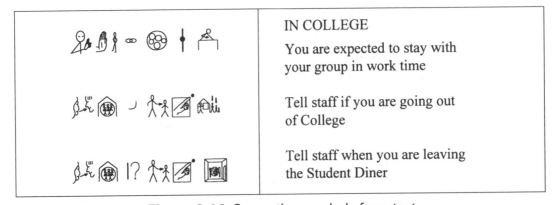

Figure 6.14 *Separating symbols from text*

Students also use symbols to help them understand and take part in the more formal annual reviews which take place in schools. They are asked about their work, interests, strengths, friends and what they would like to do when they leave school. Preparation for this and the formative Record of Achievement is made much easier by the use of question cards shown in Figure 3.4, p. 36. Having the question in front of them helps students to remember what they have been asked. They expand their answers as they listen to others and their understanding of what they are being asked grows.

The kind of workbooks put together by Selina and Jamie not only contribute to their assessment, they are also a very positive way of showing capability to a wider audience. Seeing positive role models of other people in a similar situation to oneself can help to raise personal expectations. At Frank Wise School, Banbury, the students have made computer-based multi-media presentations about themselves. They have used photographs, video, recorded speech, text and symbols to communicate. They are accessible to the creators and to all users at a variety of levels. The value of this approach is that the students are using tools which of themselves confer status, and are producing results which compare well with professionally developed materials.

6. Advocacy and self-advocacy

Probably the most exciting aspect of increasing the opportunities for people with a learning disability is the recognition of individual rights and needs. Having a voice, however, may not be enough. If the voice is to be heard, we have to persuade others to listen. The advocacy and self-advocacy movements aim to achieve this. Advocates work with individuals and groups to understand and represent their feelings and needs, while self-advocacy training is concerned with helping individuals to gain the skills to speak for themselves. 'The challenge for everyone working with young people with severe learning difficulties is how to make self-advocacy a reality' (Griffiths 1994).

More and more people with a learning disability are developing the confidence to say what they think, through education and especially with the support of advocacy organisations. 'The self-advocacy movement reflects their determination and their ability to find a voice' (Mittler 2001: 328). Many of the examples in this book demonstrate steps towards developing self-advocacy skills, and celebrating individual achievement.

The newspaper made by students at George Hastwell School does more than provide a learning opportunity. It is giving those students a voice. In showing the wider world what they can do, it enables them to present themselves in a very positive light.

At a very practical level there are many organisations supporting advocacy, self-advocacy and 'speaking up' skills. An example of the type that uses symbols in a very simple and accessible manor is the Advocacy Workbook and video pack for people with learning difficulties (BILD 2001). This uses the approach of a single symbol used as a label or cue. Like other packs of this type, it is accompanied by guidance for teachers and carers with advice on how the information is interpreted with the user. Other advocacy organisations, such as Change and People First prefer to use illustrations rather than symbols. The illustrations are very good for conveying the meaning but are less easily used by staff and users to communicate or create their own materials. It is likely that a mixed approach might overcome this difficulty.

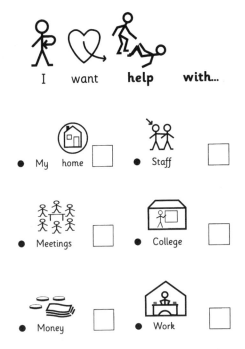

Figure 6.15 *An extract from the BILD Advocacy pack*

7. Participation

Service users are increasingly been given the right and opportunity to express views about the services they receive. This may cover a whole range of issues, their housing rights, entitlement to benefit, employment opportunities, etc. Symbols are increasingly being used to enable discussion of these issues and to present information about them. Some of the ways of doing this have already been described – using question cards as cues for answers or discussion and producing records of decisions. These need to involve the person with the learning disability to ensure that the method adopted is appropriate.

Devon has a long history of involving service users, and encouraging participation. Devon Total Communication, the Learning Disability Service, and Plymouth Community Services NHS Trust have worked together to create a wide range of information sheets written with pictures and symbols, which are described in the next chapter. They have also put a lot of effort into creating frameworks for participation in assessments and personal record-keeping.

Alongside this increased participation comes an increase in associated information, for example, in the records or reports of meetings. Here is an example of some minutes taken at a meeting between service users and social workers.

1. Lunchtimes:

It was suggested that tables could be put in the window bay during lunchtime. This would provide more seating. However, this causes further problems with where to place the snooker table.

Clients feel that although they prefer the present lay-out in the hall at lunch time, they find the queues confusing – not knowing which way to queue for the cold trolley. Staff are asked to help with this.

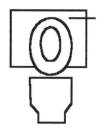

2. Toilets:

These are still not clean enough. Clients request that standards of cleaning are looked at.

Figure 6.16 *Minutes from a committee meeting*

This particular example works quite well, but is still a tricky area. There has been a considerable improvement in the quality of symbol documents. It was not so long ago that it would be common to see minutes that were not like the ones above – using symbols with discretion - but which contained huge numbers of symbols, rendering the document virtually incomprehensible to anyone, let alone part of the target audience. This topic is discussed in more depth in the next chapter.

Summary

This chapter has shown a variety of ways in which different establishments are using symbols with their students and members to develop independence. As well as finding a voice and making oneself heard, the power of the individual will be affected by what they know. One of our responsibilities, therefore, must be to make sure that as much information as possible is made accessible. This is not just a matter of making symbol or audio versions. The language, the choice of symbols and the presentation are equally important and will be considered in the next chapter.

7 Access to information

Chapter 1 identified some of the demands for more accessible information. Many organisations and centres are publishing symbol-supported information for their learning disabled members. As a result of the increase in symbol use, new issues have emerged like vocabulary selection, vocabulary development, use of language and, most importantly, the relationship between text or spoken language and symbol representation. This whole area is still new and although we can see examples of both good and bad practice, there is quite a diversity of styles and views on how information can be successfully supported. The intention behind this chapter is to promote discussion on the opportunities and constraints inherent in using symbols to create accessible information.

1. What is happening now

A very wide range of organisations, at both local and national level, use symbols as part of their strategy for involving their customers and making information more accessible. This may include an iconic use of symbols, where a document contains a few symbols to cue the reader into the topic of the document, specific paragraphs with symbols, through to documents that have very significant amounts of symbols, where the publisher clearly hopes the reader will be able to understand the full meaning of the text by reading the symbols.

There is also a clear desire to move towards a measure of consistency in the images used, for example, an NHS Trust is incorporating symbols in notices and information leaflets and is starting to include modified versions of these symbols on the general signage around the hospital instead of the previous 'designed' icons. In other Trusts symbols are gradually extending the amount of advice and guidance for patients with learning difficulties. Although the range of symbols is becoming quite extensive, there is no consistent source of illustrations as yet, and organisations are having to produce their own drawings.

Figure 7.1 *A customer satisfaction leaflet from Ravensbourne NHS Trust*

Other authorities include Humberside Health Trust, who produced the Patient's Charter with photographs and symbols plus line drawings of manual signs so that a wider range of customers might become aware of their entitlements.

There are two key questions: first, for whom is the symbol support intended? And, second, what are the circumstances in which the material will be received?

Not all users will be familiar with symbols and will need to have them explained by carers. In those cases the most successful type of solution might be similar to the one shown in Figure 7.1 with each text item supported by a single image. However, as symbols are being used much more extensively in schools and FE colleges, there is a body of users who are quite familiar with symbols and who may be able to access information reasonably independently when presented and supported appropriately.

2. The complexity of the text

The information sheet Figure 7.2 (a) was displayed in a centre to tell residents what to do in case of fire. Beside it is an alternative version (Figure 7.2 (b)) of very similar information, but where the sentences have been simplified and shortened. Importantly, each idea occupies a single line. The original document was made with the text showing, but the illustrations show them with the text hidden, to see how it might be perceived by somebody for whom the text means nothing. A reader who does not follow the text line will not be aware of the punctuation, such as full stops, marking the end of one idea and the start of another. In this respect layout is critical to readability.

Figure 7.2 *(a) Symbol information*

Figure 7.2 *(b) The same information modified so that each sentence is on a separate line*

3. The relationship between the symbol and the text

In the same way that a symbol cannot teach a concept, but merely remind the reader of a concept already understood, so information that is supported by symbols can only be accessible if the basic information itself is accessible. The level of the content has to be appropriate to the user. The language needs to be plain, ideally with no more than two or three concepts in a sentence.

The relationship between the symbol and the text is significant, and different readers will be able to handle different types of presentation. There are many examples of different styles of document. Here are three examples that explain the principles.

These examples were taken from the minutes of a committee meeting.

Example 1:

 At the committee meeting some people said that we needed a new minibus because more people wanted to be able to go out on shopping trips. We need to raise money to get a new minibus.

 We talked about how we could do this, like having Bring and Buy sales. Anne and Peter will ask members of the centre if they have ideas for raising money.

Figure 7.3 *Information with reasonably complete text with the key concepts illustrated with symbols*

This style of information is suited to documents that need to have a large amount of information, or rather complex information which will have to be mediated in any case.

Example 2:

Figure 7.4 *This has simplified text that summarises the minute, and has symbols added for the key information-carrying words*

Example 3:

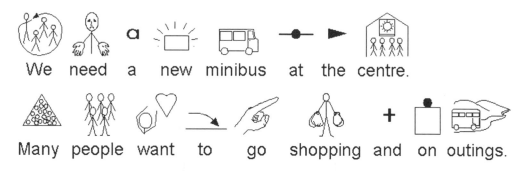

Figure 7.5 *Information in short sentences, with a symbol for each major word used*

This example will be longer than the second, and will have each major word supported. This is appropriate for users who are familiar with symbol texts. To create this type of document the author will need to be very familiar with the symbol vocabularies, in order that the most appropriate symbol is selected. This style is the one most likely to be able to be read independently by a symbol reader, as it contains the complete information.

4. How is the information to be read?

A key factor in deciding the presentational style of information is how it is likely to be read. If the information will be mediated by a carer, then the symbol cues, as in example 1, may be the most appropriate. The reader has few images to cope with, and these will act as a cue or reminder of the general topics. Where the information is intended to be made for an independent symbol reader, the style is likely to be similar to example 3.

Whichever style of presentation is chosen, care is needed with the lay-out. The symbol reader who is not looking at the text line will not see punctuation marks in the text line, and therefore will not see any division between sentences. This means that each sentence or new idea must be placed on a separate line. It may also be easier to read if there are line spaces between each sentence, so that each idea is clearly separate.

It is essential that any graphic used represents the idea being conveyed. The writer will not only need to choose between the given alternatives, but may also want to rename existing symbols in order to retain the original text, but use the most relevant symbols. An example of this is seen in example 3 above. When that document was written, there was no symbol available for the word 'outings', however, there was a symbol for the word 'trip'. They are virtually synonyms in this context and so it was absolutely appropriate to re-name the symbol for this document. While it is essential that the graphics are the most appropriate, however the information is presented, when the reader may be accessing it on computer, and hearing the text spoken, then the text line also needs to have the words that the reader is most familar with.

The second example shown was written as a plain text document and then the necessary symbols were added to support the essential concepts. Although less visually satisfactory than examples 1 and 3, this technique is much less prone to error and over-symbolisation, and may be the easiest for writers who are new to writing information with symbols.

5. Recent history

There have been a few key events in the debate about accessible information. The first of these was in 1996, at a conference entitled 'Getting it Clear' (organised by Mencap and Westminster College, Oxford) where organisations and users concerned with accessible information, came together to discuss current issues. This conference made a number of recommendations. Among these recommendations are four that are relevant to this chapter:

1   A need to develop the understanding and use of symbols, including greater understanding about appropriate levels of symbols and language for different audiences.
2   A debate on the development of symbol libraries, on the merits of having nationally agreed standards in symbols and how this might co-exist with the need for personal, local or regional symbols.
3   Involvement of symbol users in the development of accessible information. Strong feelings were expressed about the consultation and involvement of learning disabled users in initiatives set up for their benefit.
4   The final recommendation was for opportunities to share information and prevent a duplication of effort.

This last point was also the stimulus for the first edition of this book: to share current information and practice and to raise the discussion in a public forum.

Each of the subsequent events, such as the Kings Fund Conference in 1999 and the Symbol Conferences at Meldreth Manor School in 1999 and 2000 have advanced the debate and shown each of these issues gaining in importance. Although there are still examples of poor quality information being 'symbolised' and inappropriate levels of symbols, these are, thankfully, becoming much less common. There is also a greater understanding of the differences between public information, where the author has no knowledge of the reader or level of mediation, and local or organisational information where the authors are likely to be familiar with their audiences.

6. Examples of information

The rest of this chapter will look at a number of examples and attempt to give some pointers that might help others in creating their own accessible information. There are examples throughout this book which demonstrate some of the issues of using symbols for communication. These examples have been taken from many different people working in a range of contexts. Many of them show positive ways in which symbols can help, but some also illustrate the pitfalls of making good communication, as the perceptive reader may have noticed. This section discusses these points.

Local organisations

These are situations where the publisher knows the readers and their likely level of familiarity with symbols and where the readers are likely to be familiar with the issues under discussion.

Ideally, at this level there will be some user involvement in creating the information or deciding on the symbols used. The members of the Symbols Project at Borehamwood Day Centre asked if they could have a timetable which they could understand to replace the typewritten one. Members discussed how each option would be represented and chose or suggested suitable symbols (Figure 7.6). They would sit with a member of staff who was able to use the drawing package on the computer. Since this use was to be confined to a single establishment, it was totally appropriate that they should agree their own representations. Sally Paveley, reporting on the outcomes of this initiative, observed that there was a significant increase in the range of options that some of the clients would attempt. It seemed that before the options were presented in an accessible form there was a tendency for members to stick to the same familiar activities; they could not envisage the choices open to them.

Figure 7.6 *The activities timetable from Boreham Wood Day Centre*

The complexity of a solution will depend upon the ability of the users and their familiarity with the symbols. Some users will find symbols give support to an otherwise complex timetable. For other students this will be too complex, and the timetable may need issuing to them on a daily basis with just the events for that day shown in sequence.

Information from regional or larger organisations

This is information where readers may be at a variety of levels but where there is some common practice, for example, within a health authority or education authority and where the reader will have some support in accessing the content. It will still be necessary to consider the 'typical' reader and to present the information so that it is accessible to the widest group.

A doctor's surgery in Cambridgeshire has started to provide information in symbol form for patients with learning difficulties who are not able to read the information available in print. It would have been unrealistic to expect the patients to be familiar with all the symbols, and so the intention was to convey the main subject matter of the notice, so that it is possible to ask for further information. For this purpose the symbols need to be pictorial or representational, perhaps supported by photographs, drawings or even product labels. The surgery displayed a large symbol for 'ask' with a photograph of the person to ask. The member of staff responding to an enquiry is able to explain the symbols used in the notice, and provide a copy of the notice for the patient to take away and use as an *aide-mémoire*. The intention is to help the patients to become familiar with relevant symbols over a period of time. All this will not happen easily, and a long-term strategy is needed.

'The Reporter' is a newsletter produced by members of Bassetts Centre, in Farnborough. Many of the group are text readers, but some symbols are used to include others. This page on the benefits of quitting smoking are from the March 2001 edition, and illustrate a sensitive and appropriate use of symbols for a mixed audience.

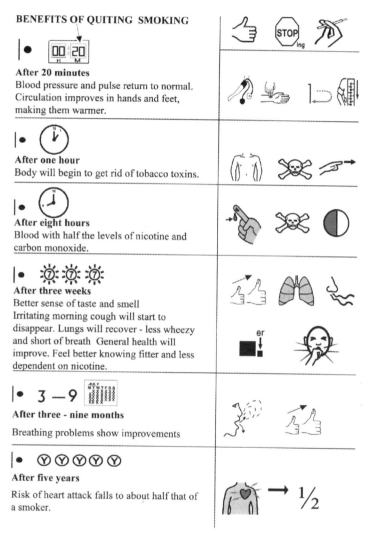

Figure 7.7 *An appropriate use of symbols to support information for a mixed audience*

One very successful format is the mixture of symbols and photographs. The photographs communicate images with which the reader can identify. They can also communicate attitude. Short symbols sentences using as concrete a vocabulary as possible can then give necessary detailed information. Gela Griffiths, formerly from Redbridge High School, worked with colleagues to create a range of careers materials including booklets that informed students about the possibilities that may be available when they leave school. The illustration in Figure 7.8 is from a booklet about going to college. The lay-out is clear and uncluttered. However, care has been taken to make it look professional.

Figure 7.8 *An information booklet with clear message and clear layout*

Public information where the publisher has no link with the audience

Of the many types of information that are produced with symbol support, the one that appears most fraught with danger is the organisational mission or policy statement. It is understandable why this is such a high priority for an organisation. Quite rightly, they want to say, 'Here we are, this is what we do, this is what we believe in, and look, we are making this information accessible to all of our service users.' Sadly, this is not always what such statements do, particularly when they are translated into a form that has symbol support.

As part of a training session, an advocacy group decided to put their mission statement into symbol form. As a first step, Mike, an outsider to the group, read each sentence and said what he thought it meant in plain English. In many cases, this did not agree with what the author had intended. Much of the vocabulary used in the original mission statement had taken on localised meanings. These nuances had grown up in the establishment over a period of time and people within the organisation were unaware of the way the use of language had become institutionalised. It was not so much that there was particular jargon, more that the use of ordinary words had become contextualised implicitly and thus carried shades of meaning that the outsider would be unaware of. It became apparent that the mission statement needed to be rewritten to make it clear to all readers, not just so that it could be supported with symbols. In this way the process of symbolising text can also provide an opportunity to reappraise the original language.

There is now much experience of symbols available and long documents full of symbols, many of which are abstract, and with many gaps where there are words that do not have symbols, are fortunately becoming much less common.

A prerequisite, therefore, in making information accessible by use of symbols, is to make it accessible in words. This is not easy, but if the initial text is unclear, a version in symbols will be even less understandable.

Considering the audience

Where the readers are known to the author, it may be a fairly straightforward job to provide symbol support for any document. The level of language, the range of symbols and the degree of symbol support needed will be known. Often, however, information needs to be prepared for a group of readers or for more public consumption. It is often not a realistic proposition to differentiate materials for different clients/students and in this case some general principles have to be established before starting work.

7. Information on the web

At the time of writing there is very little information for symbol readers on the web. However, the advances in software that allow pages of HTML to be created mean that more material will soon start to appear. This will really allow symbol users to become publishers in their own right. In the meantime, however, there are a number of key organisations that are pioneering this field. For example, Toby Homes, an organisation that cares for and runs housing for people with learning disabilities, set up a website with information and pictures for their members and potential residents.

Similarly, Information Resources for Adults with Learning Disabilities (IRALD) includes a section for users. They say:

> The Signpost home page is part of an experiment exploring the ways adults with learning disabilities can access information through an IT medium such as the World Wide Web. There are currently no provisions for this group of society to control or select information about the facilities in their local areas - or indeed on a national scale ... [And] are using the Glebe House Project as a basis for research into the practical use of web pages by carers and clients themselves. (From the home page of the Signpost project)

On the website there are sections about specific centres and also more general information on health care, such as visiting the dentist, or having your eyes tested. These pages use the presentation style as described above used by Gela Griffiths (Figure 7.8), with photographs and symbol/text captions.

Meldreth Manor school, certainly a pioneer in putting symbols on the web, has created a site which can be used with switch access for pupils who have physical difficulties. David Banes and Richard Walters, who devised the site, first identified the key features of accessibility, such as having icons in consistent places that were easy to find, and required the minimum amount of mouse movement. Later they added switch access for non-keyboard/mouse users. This site won the first of the Microsoft 'Road Ahead' awards for innovation in educational web design.

These initiatives have been taken further in a project by Tools for Inclusion and the Rara Avis Rainforest. The main Rara Avis site is written in text for more able students, and a parallel site with symbol support was created to enable participation by pupils who found reading the English text difficult. This site has switch access and simplified navigation for users who have learning difficulties. The text from the main site was simplified into short sentences, each presenting one main idea. The text was constructed so that as far as possible, the symbol information remained on a single line. This site is also accessible by switches as well as mouse or keyboard.

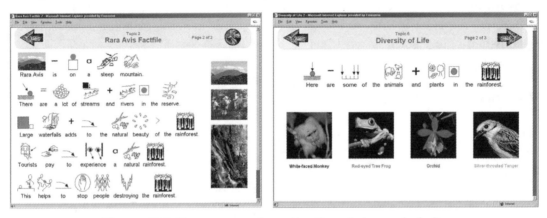

Figure 7.9 *Two screens from the Rara Avis symbol site*

One of the important considerations regarding this material is that it offers serious high quality information to learners who may be helped by symbols. There is still a real shortage of material that deals with adult topics, and which does not water down the concepts. The site www.symbolworld.org has been created especially to provide a focus for switch-accessible symbol material. There are other websites that have material for symbol users.

The web is also being used in closed groups as a means of people keeping in touch in projects or group activities. The Slice project involves one or two schools for pupils with serious communication difficulties from Bradford, Antwerp, Odense, Birmingham and Helsinki. It is looking at the use of email between teachers and pupils in these schools. The system will enable children and young people from ethnic minority backgrounds with a range of communication difficulties to communicate via email and the Internet. A website was set up to share guidelines and case studies and pro-active dissemination. Being an informal medium, the website can be used to encourage participants, teachers and students to share contributions. They are using the email program Inter_Comm which will send and receive email messages in the student's preferred symbol set. The email software will handle the translation of emails between students, but a variety of languages will be displayed on the website. It will be interesting to see the extent to which readers in different languages will be able to read the symbols without understanding the supporting text.

Figure 7.10 *The web being used to share information internationally*

Here are some web addresses for some of the sites mentioned:

Toby Homes   http://www.tobyhomes.freeserve.co.uk/
IRALD Signpost project   http://www.u-net.com/irald/signpost.htm
Meldreth Manor School   http://atschool.eduweb.co.uk/meldreth/
Rara Avis Rainforest   http://www.widgit.com/rainforest/html/start.htm or
                            http://www.ioe.ac.uk/nof/tfi/rainforest/
Symbol users' site   http://www.symbolworld.org

Summary

Creating information which is clear and accurate in symbol form is not easy. It requires training and careful thought. It also requires collaboration not only between professionals, but should also involve the users wherever possible.

The examples in this book have come from many different users, with varying degrees of experience, and different views about symbol use. It will be apparent that the use of symbols as a tool for information is very much in its infancy. Each new initiative is revealing more about what works and where the problems lie. It is important that we evaluate these attempts constructively so that we can identify where symbols are of value, and where alternative strategies may be more appropriate. Some of the lessons and their implications are discussed in the final chapter, which draws together issues for the future.

8 Issues for the future

This book has shown how practitioners are using symbols to meet the individual entitlement of pupils and adults to communication and learning. As well as showing a rich variety of approaches, it has highlighted the need for caution in symbol use. This chapter starts with a reminder of the imperatives behind symbol use. It then discusses some of the factors which may lie behind successful implementation. It ends by identifying areas where there is, currently, no consensus and which will require further debate.

1. Entitlement

Individual entitlement has been a recurrent theme throughout this book, even if not always explicitly stated. It has long been accepted that children with learning difficulties have a right to a high quality of education, and the major initiatives are, in the main, designed to improve that quality. There is a National Curriculum for all which enshrines the right of access. Many of the difficulties of implementation have been addressed, and as a profession teachers have much clearer ideas on how the curriculum can be delivered. There is an increasing emphasis on the inclusion of pupils within mainstream education, and although there are many arguments in that debate, the overriding principle of equality of access into an integrated society is an important theme.

Similarly, adults with learning disabilities have moved from institutional care to independent and autonomous living within a supported framework. These are all ideals that in practice may be far from perfect, but the trend is towards this and efforts are gradually increasing the reality, especially at grass-roots levels.

Teachers in schools are looking for strategies which can be used across the range of pupil need but which can be tailored to meet individual requirements, and staff in further education and post-school provision are recognising the need for tools to enhance communication, self-advocacy and independence. The use of Information and Communications Technology (ICT) is now recognised as essential in most organisations.

The rights of children and adults to express their own opinions on the provision being made for them is recognised in legislation and guidance. Implicit in this is a requirement to provide a means of expressing these opinions. Government is beginning to realise the implications of this, for example, through the Communication

Aids Project. This is providing assessment, training and resources for pupils in schools to develop their communication skills. No doubt this will extend into adult provision at some point as the political imperatives become more pressing.

Certainly, there are expectations in communities and their members of expressing and realising choice. There is a recognition of the need for information, as illustrated in the previous chapter.

It is not the purpose of this book to discuss the political issues behind this, rather, to look at them in so far as they affect the use of symbols. It should be clear by now that use of symbols has an impact on enabling these rights. Symbols are one of the information media that can be combined to increase access to:

- learning
- information
- independence
- self-expression
- personal growth.

There are particular features of symbols which enable them to contribute to these areas:

- They are written, drawn or printed so they have a permanency.
- They can, like pictures and text, be revisited any number of times at the pace the users wants. This is different from sound and video which are more ephemeral but also, of course, have different uses and advantages.
- The means of production and processing of symbols is comparatively cheap. At one level, for someone who can draw, this may involve just a pen and pencil. Computers and computer software that manipulates symbols are becoming common and more affordable.
- Symbols of the type described in this book are fairly accessible and many are easy to learn due to their pictorial nature. This clearly is an advantage, but the simplicity is deceptive and issues of appropriate language as well as choice of symbols need to be considered.

Much of this book has been concerned with explaining how symbols can be used in a range of contexts. This chapter will explore some of the more general issues that can make the ideas more effective. The reader will recognise that some of the points made apply not only to symbols, but to any intervention used to increase the autonomy and learning of an individual, whereas other points are specific to symbols.

2. Attitude

The introduction of any innovation requires commitment and vision on the part of its instigators. It then needs to be critically reviewed. Lessons must be learned so that as it becomes more widespread, the practice will be well informed. This implies dissemination to, and discussion with, all those involved: users, practitioners, parents, carers and others with responsibility for users, developers and resource producers, and importantly must include managers at all levels. In the final instance acceptance will only come about if the innovations are given a fair trial and are shown to be both practical and of real value. Over the past five years there has been a very perceptible increase in symbol use.

In 1997 we were concerned about the full acceptance of the implications of these rights. It is all too easy to pay lip-service without really following through the consequences. This is a real danger where managers and senior staff do not take the time to internalise the problems, or where they look for easy or instant solutions. At that time innovation was practitioner-led, and managers were, on the whole, not yet involved. Since then the importance of communication has been recognised at all organisational levels, and within that, the value of symbols. The example of the introduction of symbols within Mencap illustrates this change in attitudes and knowledge.

The first significant event concerning the introduction of symbols was at the Mencap and Gateway national conferences in 1995 and 1996. At a strategic level it was decided to introduce symbols to the conferences, even though most of the delegates would not be familiar with them at all. The development was seen in terms of a long timescale, first to build up familiarity so that symbols did not appear odd, and then to gradually increase people's understanding of symbols so that they become less dependent on support from another person. There were very different reactions to this throughout the organisation. At grass-roots level there was both concern and mistrust because it was perceived that symbols were being introduced as a panacea, and that their introduction should have started within the small local groups before moving to organisational level. On the other hand, it was also argued that putting symbols around, and making them visible was simply awareness raising. Nobody really expected that users who came to the first conferences would be able to understand this new medium. It is likely that both views were right, and in the same way that children learn to read both formally and by a process of osmosis, so symbol readers needed to see symbols in the environment as well as learning about them in their own situations.

Certainly, and not surprisingly, the improved quality of practice has had a major impact on attitude. The attitude of society towards people with disabilities is slowly changing, although there are still many people with little or no experience of being with learning disabled people. There is no longer such a stigma about using symbols as an aid to information as much as complete lack of understanding. As more centres such as the doctor's surgery in Cambridgeshire (Chapter 7) make symbols part of the ordinary environment, so symbols will be seen as more acceptable.

However, the use of symbols can be a difficult issue for parents. Whereas a child with a severe learning or communication difficulty may be relieved and even overjoyed at the possibilities offered by symbols, parents of children with less severe problems, but who may benefit from symbols as a prompt or transition to standard text, may be upset or worried at what could be seen as 'labelling'. Parents of a child with learning difficulties might initially be disappointed at the sight of symbols around a school. They may expect a traditional approach to literacy where they are familiar with the methods and thus understand its status. They want their child to learn to read and write in traditionally accepted ways. The school will need to explain that this is the goal for all children, but that some will need a lot of support through that process. Experience has shown that when parents see their child gradually acquiring skills, their preconceptions are modified, and they start to take a pride in achievements rather than showing disappointment at unmet goals. If we are serious about inclusion for all in education and society, then different means of communication must become more common.

Many organisations produce their own symbol-supported materials which are circulated locally, and some publications such as this one and *Symbols Now* (Abbott 2000) have helped to spread the examples and debates more widely.

The issues that concern us have necessarily changed. Issues such as the opportunity to write, to access adequate vocabularies, to be able to choose what to say freely and easily and to communicate with as wide a community as possible. In short, we are looking now to ensure that we as professionals or developers of solutions are not the people creating boundaries or restrictions.

3. Vocabulary

There are two aspects of vocabulary that need to be considered: first the formal vocabulary for developing literacy and learning. This is likely to be fairly small, focusing on images and concepts at the level appropriate to the learning of the user. The choice of images will depend on the user and their context. Some will prefer coloured symbols, others black and white. The inclusion of photographs and illustrations or clip-art has already been discussed. These symbols are taught and learned slowly.

However, this approach addresses only one side of the communication picture. The events of 11 September demonstrated a very important issue about access to vocabulary. The second aspect to consider is, if we focus only on the functional vocabulary we have no tools for suddenly talking about the immediate and important topics that arise. Just because a person has a cognitive difficulty does not mean they cannot or do not want to discuss the events in front of them or on the news. The grid in Figure 8.1 was made very rapidly as a tool for discussion and explanation when the Queen Mother died.

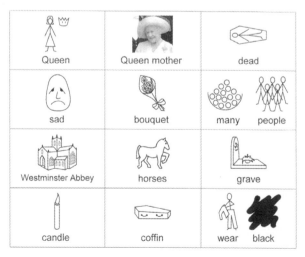

Figure 8.1 *A grid for discussion – made the moment it was needed*

Grids like this, although not perfect, can facilitate a discussion. Even though some of the symbols may be new, because they are used in context they can be more easily explained. This also illustrates the importance of technology – being able to make this instantly as need arises. It also shows that while most of the vocabulary may remain unused, its availability can (and should) make a major difference.

At the time of the first edition of *Literacy Through Symbols* there was great discussion on symbols themselves, whether there should be a single national standard, whether organisations should be encouraged to develop their own symbols. We have seen both a relaxation of the nervousness about this issue, and a more pragmatic approach prevailing. More people are being involved in the development and design of symbols, and so there is greater confidence in the actual images being used. The Rebus Symbol Development Project involved a network of professionals and users to check and validate the designs. This approach is essential if the images are to meet real need rather than perceived need or tokenism.

4. Tools for writing

Currently the tools that we have for writing favour the person who can type. They are fine for creating symbol-supported materials for users to read. At the time of writing, there are various software programs around which enable pictures to be pasted into a document. Writing with Symbols 2000 has the additional language support enabling a choice of images according to the meaning and context. But the on-screen grids are limited. Grids need to be created before a writer can start, and the vocabulary is restricted to fairly small numbers of images available on the set of grids. There are dynamic sets of grids available, such as the Chailey vocabulary and the Ingfield vocabulary sets, but their structure is along the lines of a communication aid, for direct communication rather than for writing. No doubt this will start to change in the near future. In the meantime the commonly used strategy of co-creation, where a writer is helped, gives limited access to freedom of speech. It is essential that helpers working in this way take great care to facilitate and not to direct.

The issue for the future is to devise technologies that can offer real freedom in writing, for example, context-sensitive help, graphic prediction, and systems that will learn the way that individuals write. The example of the discussion grid on the death of the Queen Mother illustrates how users can assimilate new vocabulary in context. Systems need to accommodate both the standard vocabulary a user requires as well as enabling access to new topics.

5. Changing horizons

Access to information, newsletters and messages has certainly opened horizons for many people with learning disabilities. Email is starting to extend these horizons. Johanna Frohm (Chapter 1) helps her son in the USA write letters to Rebecca (Chapter 1). They have never met, but really enjoy receiving and sending letters to each other. It is interesting to note that Mike Frohm uses PCS Symbols and Rebecca uses Rebus symbols, but that seems to create little difficulty for these two, especially as they are each supported in their reading and writing. The creation and reading process may not be entirely independent, but this exchange of ideas widened their horizons.

Email will allow a writer to create messages in symbols and send them to another symbol reader. The same message sent to a standard email program will be seen as text, but the reply, from the text writer, will be interpreted as symbols back in the symbol software. Email is being used to keep family members in touch. As we become more familiar with the technologies it will inevitably increase opportunities for correspondence.

The challenge is to change the focus from symbol users being the recipients of information to being creators.

6. Research

There is now a very large body of anecdotal evidence of the impact that symbols can have on some individuals, as shown in this book and *Symbols Now* (Abbott 2000). There are still very few rigorous studies of this effectiveness, and few answers that might guide us on the most effective ways of enhancing literacy through graphic support. Current research still focuses on symbols used as an aid for direct face-to-face communication, and we understand very little of the different strategies that could be adopted for literacy.

A number of small action research studies have been undertaken by teachers under their professional development, but few of these ever reach the public arena, or are even shared informally. There are issues here for institutes of higher education and teacher education as well as in speech and language therapy. Sound research would inform us all, ensuring that we were making genuine steps, not just being tokenistic. It would help software, hardware and resource developers to create more effective tools, which in turn could help to consolidate the changes in attitude that we are all seeking – changes in attitude towards people with learning or communication difficulties, and changes in expectations and aspirations by everybody.

Postscript

In writing this book we have wanted to increase awareness of just how effective symbols can be as a communication tool for people with a learning disability. During the time that we have worked with symbols, exploring their use across all phases, we have seen a change in the fundamental attitudes to people with learning disabilities. Even allowing for some degree of lip-service in all this, at least the right things are (generally) being said, and where problems are internalised, this has led to enormous advances in the use of symbols and other methods used to help autonomy and learning.

There is a political imperative and climate to move forward and however political attitudes might change, it seems that this development is now unstoppable. Once people have found their voice, it is almost impossible to take it away. Those instances which have given us most pleasure, seeing children involved in the curriculum without the frustration of not being able to read and write text; a parent in tears when their 12-year-old brought something home for the first time that he could read; Reg, in his forties standing up for the first time and reading, albeit with help, about how he won the photography competition; and Mike and Rebecca whose stories started this book – all these should become more and more common as children and adults with learning disabilities take a more active role in society. We hope this book on symbols will make a small, but nonetheless significant, contribution to that process.

References

Abbott, C. (2000) *Symbols Now*, Leamington Spa, Widgit Software Ltd.

Allen, J., Cockerill, H., Davies, E. *et al.* (1992) *Augmentative Communication: More than Just Words*, Oxford, ACE Centre.

Amos, J. (1995) *Feelings*, Slough, Cherrytree Press Ltd.

Berenstein, S. and Berenstein, J. (1972) *Bears in the Night*, Glasgow, Collins.

Bovair, K. and Robbins, B. (1996) 'Modern foreign languages', in Carpenter, B., Ashdown, R. and Bovair, K. (eds) *Enabling Access*, London, David Fulton, pp. 108–22.

Brown, E. (1996) 'Religious education', in Carpenter, B., Ashdown, R. and Bovair, K. (eds) *Enabling Access*, London, David Fulton, pp. 147–65.

Brown, E. (1999) *Loss, Change and Grief*, London, David Fulton Publishers.

Carle, E. (1970) *The Very Hungry Caterpillar*, London, Puffin Books.

Carpenter, B. (1995) 'Self-assessment using symbols', in *Extending Horizons*, Derbyshire, Imagination Technology.

Carpenter, B. and Morris, D. (2001) 'Perspectives on the National Curriculum: English', in Carpenter, B., Ashdown, R. and Bovair, K. (eds) *Enabling Access* (2nd edn), London, David Fulton, pp. 15–35.

Corker, J. and Rice, J. (1996) *Finding a Voice*, Rotherham, Honormead Schools.

Cregan, A. (1982) *Sigsymbol Dictionary/Teaching Pack*, Hatfield, Herts.

Curriculum Council for Wales (1991) *Teacher Support Programme: Teaching History to Pupils with Severe and Moderate Learning Difficulties*, Cardiff.

Department of Health (2001) *Valuing People: A New Strategy for Learning Disability in the 21st Century*, London, The Stationery Office, March.

Devereux, K. and van Oosterom, J. (1984) *Learning with Rebuses*, Stratford-upon-Avon, National Council for Special Education.

DFE (1994) *Code of Practice on the Identification and Assessment of Special Educational Needs*, London, HMSO.

DfES/QCA (2001) *Planning, Teaching and Assessing the Curriculum for Pupils with Learning Difficulties*, London, Qualifications and Curriculum Authority.

Goosens, C., Crain, S. and Elder, P. (1992) 'Engineering the pre-school environment for interactive, symbolic communication: 18 months to 5 years developmentally'. S.E. AC Conference Publications, 2430 11th Avenue North, Birmingham, AL 35234.

Griffiths, M. (1994) *Transition to Adulthood*, London, David Fulton.

Grove, N. (1998) *Literature for All*, London, David Fulton.

Gummett, B. and Martin, C. (2001) 'Geography' in Carpenter, B. *et al.* (eds) *Enabling Access* (2nd edn), London, David Fulton, pp. 90–9.

James, F. (1993) 'Reading – a door to independence', in van Oosterom *et al.*, *Symbols in Practice*, Coventry, NCET.

James, F. and Kerr, A. (1993) *On First Reading: Ideas for Developing Reading Skills with Children from Four to Seven*, Twickenham, Belair Publications Ltd.

Jones, P. and Cregan, A. (1986) *Sign and Symbol Communication for Mentally Handicapped People*, London, Croom Helm.

Kiernan, C., Reid, B. and Goldbart, J. (1987) *Foundations of Communication and Language. Course Manual*, Manchester, Manchester University Press in association with the British Institute of Mental Handicap.

King-DeBaun, P. (1990) *Storytime*, Georgia, Acworth.

Lloyd, G. (1996) Unpublished report of work at Woodlands School.

Lonke, F., Clibbins, J., Arvidson, H. and Lloyd, L. (1999) *Augmentative and Alternative Communication: New Directions in Research and Practice*, London, Whurr Press.

Martin, C. and Gummett, B. (2001) 'History', in Carpenter, B. *et al.* (eds) *Enabling Access* (2nd edn), London, David Fulton, pp. 80–9.

McNamara, S. and Moreton, G. (1990) *Teaching Special Needs*, London, David Fulton.

Mittler, P. (2001) 'Preparing for Self-advocacy', in Carpenter, B. *et al.* (eds) *Enabling Access* (2nd edn), London, David Fulton, pp. 328–45.

Nunes da Ponte, M. (1996) 'Encouraging communication: encouraging communication for young disabled children', unpublished paper presented at Westminster College, Oxford.

Parker, M. and Wright, C. (1991) 'Using Rebus symbols', unpublished project report 15 November, Ysgol Erw'r Delyn, South Glamorgan.

Paveley, S. (1993) *Self-Respect and Independence*, Coventry, NCET.

Richle, J., York, J. and Sigafoos, J. (1991) *Implementing Augmentative and Alternative Communication*, Baltimore, MD, Paul H. Brooks Publishing Company.

Schlosser, R. (1997) 'Nomenclature of category levels in graphic symbols, part 1: is a flower a flower a flower?', *AAC Augmentative and Alternative Communication*, vol. 13, March, pp. 4–13.

Symbol Users Advisory Group (1994) *An Introduction to Picture Sets and Symbol Systems*, Oxford, ACE Centre.

van Oosterom, J. and Devereux, K. (1992) *Rebus Glossary*, Cambridge, LDA.

Materials, information and suppliers

Web addresses

Information about symbols

www.widgit.com – publisher of Writing with Symbols 2000 and the Rebus Symbols
www.makaton.org – publishers of Makaton Signs and symbol resources
www.mayer-johnson.com – publishers of PCS Symbols and Boardmaker
http://www.mycommlink.info – a site created by a parent to share ideas
http://www.compic.com – publishers of compic symbols
http://www-cod.csun.edu – useful articles for the CSUN conference
http://www.closingthegap.com – forum from the Closing the Gap Conference
www.inclusive.co.uk – information pages, plus suppliers of software, peripherals, training and
http://rehabengineer.homestead.com – information on symbols and other relevant materials
http://www.communicationmatters.org.uk – information on AAC

On-line materials for symbol users

Symbol users' site	http://www.symbolworld.org
Toby Homes	http://www.tobyhomes.freeserve.co.uk/
IRALD Signpost project	http://www.u-net.com/irald/signpost.htm
Meldreth Manor School	http://atschool.eduweb.co.uk/meldreth/
Rara Avis Rainforest	http://www.widgit.com/rainforest/html/start.htm
	or http://www.ioe.ac.uk/nof/tfi/rainforest/

Suppliers of symbol sets

Blissymbolics Communication International,
Lawrence Avenue West,
Suite 104,
Toronto, M6L IC5
Ontario,
Canada
tel. 416 242 9114,
or Blissymbol Communication UK,
ACE Centre (address below on p. 119)

Compic Symbols,
Compic Development Association,
PO Box 351,
Balwyn,
Victoria 3104,
Australia
tel. 62 3 857 8151

Makaton sign graphics and symbols,
Makaton Vocabulary Development Project,
31 Firwood Drive,
Camberley,
Surrey GU15 3QD
tel. 01276 61390
email mvdp@makaton.org
web: www.makaton.org

PCS Symbols,
Mayer-Johnson Co.,
Box 1579,
Solana Beach
CA 92075-1579,
USA
tel. 619 550-0449
email mayerj@mayer-johnson.com
web www.mayer-johnson.com

PIC Symbols,
SIH Laromedal Umea,
Mariehemsvagen 2,
S-906 54,
Umea,
Sweden
tel. 46 90 13 9140

Widgit Rebus Symbols,
Widgit Software Ltd,
124 Cambridge Science Park,
Milton Road,
Cambridge CB4 0ZS,
tel. 01223 425558,
email info@widgit.com
web www.widgit.com

Software

Writing with Symbols 2000, Complete and Inter_Comm, from Widgit Software Ltd
Boardmaker, available from Widgit Software Ltd
Makaton sign graphics and symbols from MVDP
Clicker range – PCS and Makaton Symbols can be bought separately to use with this, from Crick Software Ltd
Microsoft Powerpoint – useful for making interactive symbol resources
Concept Multimedia – for Overlay Keyboards and utility software, from The Advisor Unit, Hatfield

Useful addresses and suppliers

ACE Centre Advisory Trust,
92 Windmill Road,
Headington,
Oxford OX3 7DR
tel. 01865 759800
email info@ace-centre.org.uk
URL http://www.ace-centre.org.uk

ACE Centre-North,
1 Broadbent Road,
Watersheddings,
Oldham OLI 4LB,
tel. 0161 627 1358
email acenorth@ace-north.org.uk
URL http://www.ace-north.org.uk

AU: Computers in Education,
126 Great North Road,
Hatfield,
Herts AL9 5JZ,
tel. 01707 266714
email sallyp@advisory-unit.org.uk
web URL http://www.advisory-unit.org.uk

Asdan,
Wainbrook House,
Hudds Vale Road,
St George,
Bristol BS5 7HY
tel. 0117 9411126
email info@asdan.co.uk
URL http://www.asdan.co.uk

Becta (British Educational Communications and Technology Agency),
Milburn Hill Road,
Science Park,
Coventry CV4 7JJ
tel. 0124 7641 6994
URL http://www.becta.org.uk

BILD,
Campion House,
Green Street,
Kidderminster,
Worcestershire DY10 1JL,
tel. 01562 723010
email enquiries@bild.org.uk
URL http://www.bild.org.uk

CALL Centre (Communication Aids for Language and Learning),
University of Edinburgh,
Patersons Lane,
Holyrood Road,
Edinburgh EH8 8AQ
tel. 0131 651 6235
email call-centre@ed.ac.uk
URL http://callcentre.education.ed.ac.uk

CENMAC (Centre for Micro-Assisted Communication),
Charlton Park School,
Charlton Park Road,
London SE7 8JB
tel. 020 8854 1019
email cenmac@cenmac.greenwich.gov.uk
URL http://www.cenmac.demon.co.uk

Communication Matters,
c/o ACE Centre,
93 Windmill Road,
Headington,
Oxford OX3 7DR
tel. 0870 606 5463
email admin@communicationmatters.org.uk
URL http://www.communicationmatters.org.uk

Crick Software Ltd,
35 Charter Gate,
Quarry Park Close,
Moulton Park,
Northampton NN3 6QB
tel. 01604 671691
email info@cricksoft.com
URL http://www.cricksoft.com/

E & G Publications,
'Linbu',
The Crescent,
Grange-Over-Sands,
Cumbria LA11 6AW
tel. 01539 535016
email George@lindley93.freeserve.co.uk

Inclusive Technology Ltd,
Gatehead Business Park,
Delph New Road,
Delph,
Oldham OL3 5BX
tel. 01457 819790
email inclusive@inclusive.co.uk
URL http://www.inclusive.co.uk

LDA,
Duke Street,
Wisbech,
Cambs PE13 2AE
tel. 01223 357744
email ldacustserv@mcgraw-hill.com
URL http://www.ldalearning.com

MVDP,
31 Firwood Drive,
Camberley,
Surrey GU15 3QD,
tel. 01276 61390
email mvdp@makaton.org
URL httlp:// www.makaton.org

The National Autistic Society,
393 City Road,
London EC1V 1NG
tel. 020 7833 2299
email nas@nas.org.uk
URL http://www.oneworld.org/autism_uk

Widgit Software Ltd,
124 Cambridge Science Park,
Milton Road,
Cambridge CB4 0ZS
tel. 01223 425558
email info@widgit.com
URL http://www.widgit.com